D1566096

My Three Wishes

Memoir of a Hawaiian Dancer
Whose Family Troupe Traveled the World

My Three Wishes

Memoir of a Hawaiian Dancer
Whose Family Troupe Traveled the World

Kance Kaye

Fresh Ink Group
Guntersville

My Three Wishes:
Memoir of a Hawaiian Dancer Whose
Family Troupe Traveled the World

Fresh Ink Group
An Imprint of:
The Fresh Ink Group, LLC
1021 Blount Avenue, #931
Guntersville, AL 35976
Email: info@FreshInkGroup.com
FreshInkGroup.com

Edition 1.0   2021

Book design by Amit Dey / FIG
Cover design by Stephen Geez / FIG
Associate publisher Lauren A. Smith / FIG

Cataloging-in-Publication Recommendations:
BIO026000 BIOGRAPHY & AUTOBIOGRAPHY / Personal Memoirs
PER003000 PERFORMING ARTS / Dance / General
TRV025130 TRAVEL / United States / West / Pacific (AK, CA, HI, OR, WA)

Library of Congress Control Number: 2021909418

ISBN-13: 978-1-947893-20-7 Papercover
ISBN-13: 978-1-947893-21-4 Hardcover
ISBN-13: 978-1-947893-22-1 Ebooks

Dedication

To my four beautiful children, Mataiva, Keni,
Michelle, & Keone; and my dearest sister, Carolyn,
who is now flying with the angels; and my brother,
Keoki. Special mahalo to Chuck, who believed
in me to make my wishes come true.

Acknowledgments

A special recognition and mahalo to my dear friend, Kanani Nicdao, who took this task of helping me prepare my book for publication. Kanani is a very beautiful, intelligent, and giving person who I met at the Polynesian Resort while dancing for Auntie Kau'i. She understood how important that I write and finish this book.

I wrote this book so my children and their Ohana (family) would be able to share my experiences as a child and how things have changed. Thank you to my dear friends, Yvonne D., Meleilani P., Olivia M., and Rosana P. who encouraged me to share my story about my life.

A very special mahalo to my children, Mataiva, Keni, Michelle and Keone who entertained in my group, Kanoe's Micronesian Revue, especially during the Seven Day Caribbean Cruises. Thank you for your love, patience, understanding, and fun times we experienced entertaining as a family and being a very important part of my dream.

A special mahalo to Chuck for your support, love, patience and understanding and making us a part of your family. You Rocked as a Dad and Photographer who took all the wonderful photos of our group.

Table of Contents

1

Kanoe's Story

Where do I begin my beautiful story about My Three Wishes??? I have so many memories that prepared me for this since I was a child. Let me start with "My Three Wishes" at the age 19.

My First Wish: I wanted to entertain in Japan with my Polynesian Revue

My Second Wish: I wanted to entertain on the Cruise Ships with my Polynesian Revue

My Third Wish: I wanted to work for the Airlines

After hearing all my young friends tell me when they grew up, they wanted to be just like me, my close friends, Meleilani and Olivia M., convinced me to write my book and share my wonderful experiences with my children, family and friends. Remembering all my happy thoughts as a child, I began entertaining at the age of 3 for the USO (United Service Organizations) Shows with a lot of military in the audience standing in front of our stage. I was born & raised in Honolulu,

Hawaii, and took hula lessons since I was three years old. My first performance was entertaining for the USO Show with my cousins, Sylvia & Lovena Naylor. My Mom told me that I would dance & all the sailors & audience would toss coins at me. The sound of the coins, nickels, dimes, quarters, and 50 cent pieces distracted me, and I stopped dancing and started picking up all the coins and put it into a paper cup someone handed me. After I picked up all the coins, I would start dancing again. That was the beginning of earning my own money and my love for entertaining began. The only things that I can remember about World War II were the windows of our home had to be painted black, 8:00 pm siren was our curfew for lights out and everyone had to be home. We also had gas masks for school and bomb shelters (10 x 20 feet covered with concrete, vines and grass to protect us from bombs and debris).

Lessons of Life

Let me explain to you about my childhood & how I was raised to be independent & smart. My parents were very strict!!!! I was not allowed to speak pidgin English (our local broken English) at home. Whenever I was with my cousins (cuzs) and friends and out of my home, the natural pidgin came out!!! I didn't ever answer with "what" instead of "yes" when my parents called me. I was not allowed to roll my eyes or I would get a lickin' (spanking or a slap on the side of my head). I made sure that I was obedient and didn't have to be disciplined!!! Our parents were strict; however, all of my generation that I knew turned out to be good kids. We all showed respect to everyone!!!

I went to a private Episcopal School for Girls, St. Andrews Priory, from my second thru fourth grades. I had the best penmanship in the second grade that the nuns always had me write the assignments on the board. Throughout my school years, I was always asked to write the assignments on the board and still have the prettiest printing and cursive, as I always get complimented on my beautiful penmanship. I had very good nuns that taught me to achieve this in the second grade. The difference between a private school and a public school was we went to mass every day at 10:00 am and wore uniforms which looked like a sailor's top in white with a black tie, a black pleated skirt and black & white saddle oxfords. At 12:00 noon every day, the church bells would ring, and we would all stand still and say the prayers like Hail Mary and Our Father. This usually happened during our lunch hour and while we were playing in the school courtyard. I took piano lessons from the second thru the third grades and hated reading music. I was forced to take piano lessons so that I could accompany my Dad who sang falsetto. That was a lot of pressure for me to play by notes and keep up with my Dad. I taught myself to play by ear and did it every chance I had.

My parents gave me an allowance of $7.00 a week. I didn't realize that was a lot of money at my age; however, it was to teach me how to manage my money. My allowance was to take care of my following expenses for the week & taught me how to manage my allowance wisely. We lived at Papakolea, a

Hawaiian Homes Residential Community, which is located above Punchbowl National Cemetery. At the tender age of 7, I was educated on how to use the public bus transportation, the Honolulu Rapid Transit (HRT), with bus transfers to my school in the city which cost five cents each way. How many parents today do that with their 7-year-olds??? An important point to make is today it is not safe for 7-year-olds to ride on the bus by themselves!!! Lunch was 20 cents each day, snacks of Chinese Pretzels or cookies were 10 cents for each recess and round-trip transportation also referred to as car fare which totaled to just 50 cents per day totaled to $2.50 per week.

On Saturday, I took hula lessons and had to clean the house. My chores were to sweep and mop the hardwood floors and large lauhala mat made from the coconut tree palms which covered our living room floor, clean the entire house and dust the furniture while the Hawaiian music was blaring loudly from the radio. The music was soothing and a big distraction while I was cleaning because whenever a song was played and I knew the dance, I would stop working and dance the hula. My parents couldn't figure out why it took me so long to clean the house and dancing made me very happy and was a favorite part of my life!!! They would go to buy groceries and run errands and when they came home, they would say to me, why are you taking so long to clean the house??? Oh, another distraction was I would play the piano and sing the Hawaiian songs if I didn't know the hula. My Dad played the large bass for a band on the weekends and when they were gone, I would get on his bass and play it and sing too!!! I was a happy child doing my thing while I was alone at home. I had to be sure to be done with the house before 11:00 am to be at hula class by 11:30 am.

My parents were very strict with me about going to church on Sunday which was my day off for recreation. My Dad was an Episcopalian, my Mom was a Protestant, and I was a Catholic. My Dad and Mom would alternate churches every week. If I didn't go to church, I wasn't allowed to go out for the day so no movies for me. I went to church so that I could go to the movies!!! Sounds terrible but that's what I had to do to go out on Sunday. I liked going to church, I just didn't like getting up early!!! On Sunday after church, I had $4.50 to spend on recreation or entertainment like going to the movies, lunch & shopping. Movies were 20 cents, popcorn was 10 cents, and drinks were 10 cents. After the movie, lunch was Saimin, Japanese noodles in flavored hot broth, for 20 cents & bar-be-cue on the stick at 5 cents each totaling 35 cents. If I couldn't decide between two movies, I'd go to two movies that day. Bus fare was 10 cents each way on the weekends, so my entertainment costs totaled to 60 cents for movies & bus fare and lunch was 35 cents. My weekly entertainment totaled 95 cents. I hated doing things by myself so I usually treated my girlfriend to go with me which would total to $1.90. Trust me, I didn't treat someone every week. Sometimes they would pay for their own. $2.50 for School, $1.90 Entertainment for a total of $4.40 a week which left me with $2.60 a week. I had to learn how to budget my allowance to last a week. I only got $7.00 a week & that was final-tax free.

I didn't realize how lucky I was at 7 years of age until I grew older. My children couldn't believe it either as I couldn't afford to give each child that amount when I became a parent. My daughter, Michelle, said don't tell my grandchildren about my allowance or they would ask their parents for a retro-allowance. Things were very different when I was a child since I was raised as a single child.

Sharing & Being Independent

A s a child, my Mom used to send me to the island of Kauai to spend time with my other relatives while she attended Beauty College. I was treated very well & there was no favoritism. One summer I stayed with my Aunty Gerry, Uncle August & their children Leroy, Sylvia, Wendy & Elithe. My Aunt & Uncle owned a group of homes that they rented to the sugar cane workers which was called the camp. We played with their children and one incident that I remembered my cousins, Wendy, Elithe and I caught some ukus (lice) and when we got home, Aunty Gerry poured kerosene on our heads & wrapped our heads in a nylon stocking. Yep, that's how it was handled when we were kids. I was going in the 4th grade after summer. Aunty Gerry also owned a Bakery and every day she would bring home lemon meringue, chocolate meringue, apple & custard pies, breads, rolls, etc. that wasn't sold that day. Thank, God, I was an active child & burned up the calories & didn't gain a pound!!! That summer my Aunt's relatives (25 total) all flew up to Kauai from Honolulu for the summer and shipped their weapons carrier (a military vehicle that is a truck similar to an oversized jeep that was designed to carry mortars or machine guns and their crews. It carried 6-8 people on each side in the rear when we used it) and we did a lot of sightseeing. We visited places like Wailua River & Falls, Fern Grotto, Waipahee Falls (Slippery Slide), Waimea Canyon which is similar to our Grand Canyon, Menehune Pond, Wet & Dry Caves of Haena where you could hike up to it & swim… one with icy blue water & other with green blue water and the Dry Caves of Haena. The adults also spent the night at Nawiliwili Pier fishing all night & we played cards and slept in the weapons carrier. I remember going up to the mountains & picking delicious mountain apples & eating it right off the tree. It was fun!!!

I also stayed with my Cuz, ChaCha & parents, Aunty Annie & Uncle Freddie, Cuzs (cousins) Jocelyn, Ronnie, Sherwood, Auntie Alice & Uncle Ben; Al Nobriga, Puanani, Greg, Lei, Auntie Christie & Uncle Alfred; Rosie, Ben, Aunty Mary & Uncle Benny Napoleon; and Sonny Boy, Healani, Aunty Myrtle, & Uncle Sonny Napoleon. It was a great treat to stay and spend the summer with my Kauai cousins. I was very fortunate to spend time on Kauai with my family. If I didn't, I would have never been close to them as children and would never be close to them as adults.

During my 4th Grade, I lived with my Godparents, Aunty Verna, Uncle John, and their children Lowell, Jonathan, Gerrianne and Makana. We all had our chores. Mine was to cook rice everyday measuring the water with my finger. After you wash the rice, you use your middle finger and measure from the tip of your finger to the first line where you bend your first knuckle to measure the correct water measurement for the rice. There were no electric rice cookers at that time. My other chore was to take care of the one bathroom in our three-bedroom home. I learned to scrub the tub without a shower head, the basin and toilet with Dutch Cleanser and a sponge. Of course, I kept it sparkling clean.

Every Saturday, it was payday and our day off. We used to each get an envelope with $2.00 in it, itemizing our pay by our chores. If we didn't do our chores, we got our pay deducted. We were always good at getting our $2.00 every Saturday and Lowell and I would go to the Queens' Theatre in Kaimuki for the Porky Pig Club at 9:00 a.m. I used to play a lot of the games like musical chairs and eat a saltine cracker and be the first one to whistle. I gave the prizes that I won to Aunty Verna and remember winning a set of colorful Pyrex bowls nestled in each other. There were five bowls in bright colors of red, yellow, blue, green and orange. After the movie which costs 9 cents, we went to eat saimin for 20 cents and bar-be-cue beef on the stick for 5 cents each. During the summer of my 4th Grade, I asked my Mom if my brother, Danny Boy, 3, and I could go to the movies to see "Mr. Peabody and the Mermaid" starring Ann Blyth and William Powell. I was so intrigued with seeing a mermaid!!! Mom said no we couldn't go to the matinee. When my Mom took a nap that afternoon, Danny Boy and I ran away from home and went to the movie. Trust me, it was worth it!!! After the movie, we went to eat hamburgers, potato salad and coca cola. It was dark after we got home about 7:45 pm as 8:00 pm was the curfew for young children to be home in Honolulu. The siren blew to remind all kids they had to be home. Anyway, when we got home, there were four policemen at our home as my Mom didn't know where we were. My Uncle John came over and the entire family was afraid when he showed up as he was the disciplinary person for our family!!! My Mom was so glad to see us safe and welcomed us with open arms, but we got the serious lecture from Uncle John, who had the reputation of the Mafia Godfather. Of course, we cried and was afraid of him!!!

I spent my 5th Grade with my Aunty Ellen, Uncle Jimmy & cousins, Junior, Gerald, Francis, Barbara & Bobby Napoleon. We lived in a 3-bedroom home with one bathroom. Junior & Gerald attended Kamehameha School for Boys and sang a lot of Hawaiian songs. I learned all the words to several Hawaiian songs by just listening to them & their friends jam at their home. Their friends and my cuzs Sepa, Teddy Bear and Aua all came to hang out & jam every weekend with their ukuleles, guitars & homemade bass made from a large wash tub. Staying with a lot of different relatives helped me in my growing years to be independent and able to improvise unexpected situations.

I remember going to the corner grocery store to pick up things like bread which costs 20 cents, soda was 5 cents, cigarettes for my aunt for 20 cents a pack and our family had a running tab. At the end of the month, they would pay the tab. Most of the groceries were purchased at Foodland Grocery Store, which still exists in Honolulu and also Leonard's Bakery known for their hot malasadas still located on Kapahulu Ave. I also remember hamburger sandwiches with lettuce, tomato and onion were 25 cents and a soda for 5 cents. My fave was a hamburger, soda and potato salad for lunch on the weekend.

I don't even remember having any French fries when I was young!!!

My Mom always cooked meals from scratch and always had fresh vegetables on the table. There were no fast-food places around. I hated when she cooked liver and onions!!! Yuck!!! I would rather starve than eat that. I tried and it had the consistency of a pencil eraser. We either ate what our Mom cooked, or we would starve!!! I really didn't like watercress but like it now. I remember our Mom telling us to eat everything on our dinner plate & don't waste food because a lot of children in China were starving without any food. It was cool to see the Chinese man come thru the neighborhood with a can on each end of a wooden pole over his shoulders and shout out "manapua, (red sweet pork in a steamed white bun), pepeiau (dim sum pork hash)," a cool snack for us during lunch time. Another treat time for us was when the ice cream truck came thru the neighborhood playing his music on the loudspeaker so that everyone could run home and get change to buy ice cream drumsticks, creamsicles, popsicles, etc.

When we were young, we didn't have tv so we would lay around the big family radio and listen to Roy Rogers and Dale Evans, Gene Autry, Hopalong Cassidy, the Cisco Kid, the Lone Ranger and Tonto and the Shadow Knows. When I was 8, my parents bought me a piano for my birthday, and it had a large red ribbon on the music stand on the piano. I also remember my favorite toy when I was a child was a doll that I could feed with her bottle and the doll also wet in her diaper and I got to change her. What a wonderful childhood I had!!! Oh, I also used the broom stick as a horse to play cowboys and Indians. My other most favorite Christmas gift was my girl's bike!!! That was the best!!! We didn't have any cell phones & had to be home before the street lights came on to eat dinner as a family. What great memories we had!!! Another unusual thing was having a 4-party telephone line that was shared with unknown people. If we wanted to use the phone and someone was on the phone, we would ask the person if they were going to be long on their call. The reply was usually… why, is this an emergency??? If not, they would just say to wait until they got off the phone. I would just say, okay, I'll just listen to you on your call so that I knew when the phone was available!!! Click!!! Thank you!!! Best way to have them hang up!!!

⋆ *When I shut my mouth and turn to walk away, it doesn't mean you've won. It simply means your stupid ass isn't worth any more of my time.* ⋆

Broccoli Salad

First make dressing and chill

1 c. sugar

1/2 c. good mayo (Wanda likes Dukes & Kanoe likes Hellmann's Light Mayonnaise)

1 TB. cider vinegar

- Mix together and chill

1 large head of broccoli cut in bite-size pieces

1/2 purple onion, minced

2 oz. bacon bits (Publix brand in the salad dressing aisle)

Shredded sharp cheddar cheese to taste in every bite

- Combine dressing with salad at least an hour before serving and let flavors gel. The dressing will seem very thick and not seem to be enough when you first mix together. Dressing will be thinner by the time you serve.
- Toss well and enjoy.

Make a double batch for a party. Thank you, Wanda S.P., for sharing this delicious salad!!!

Pina Colada Muffins

1 box Yellow Cake Mix

2/3 cup water

1 stick melted butter

1 small can crushed Pineapple

1/2 cup Coconut, 1 tsp. Coconut Extract

1 tsp. Rum Extract

- Combine all ingredients in a bowl
- Spray muffin tins with nonstick spray
- Fill tins halfway and bake at 350 degrees for 20-25 minutes

Crab Dip

6 oz. frozen king crab or Dungeness crab

2 TB. Hellmann's Light Mayo

4 oz. cream cheese

1/4 c. sweet round onion, chopped

4 TB. heavy cream

1 garlic clove, minced

Salt & Pepper

- Blend together.
- Put in casserole & bake at 350 degrees till bubbly or crusty on top

Really ono!!!

2

Love to Entertain

I have always loved dancing hula as far back at the tender age of 3 years old. My parents sent me to different instructors such as The Alama Sisters, (Puanani & Leilani); Ruby Ahakuelo; Joe Kahaulelio; Blossom Kaipo from Wahiawa, and last of all, John Piilani Watkins, Kumu Hula, Composer, and Musician originally from Hana, Maui. I was trained to dance the traditional hula but loved the Hawaiian style created by Johnny Watkins and have continued to perpetuate his style of dance through displaying a modern & colorful mixture of the dances of Polynesia which included Hawaiian, Maori, Samoan & Tahitian and sometimes Show Songs which I used seasonally during Christmas.

I was raised from the 6th Grade to my 8th Grade in a Hawaiian Homes Community called "Papakolea" which is located near the Punchbowl Cemetery located at Punchbowl Crater in Honolulu also known as the National Memorial Cemetery of the Pacific. I had my best childhood experience there. Any families living at Papakolea had to be part Hawaiian and all of the kids I grew up with went to the Community Hall where we learned a lot of things like craft, hula, and sports. My favorite time was during the summer when we all attended a Summer Fun Program which lasted from 10 am to 5 pm from Mondays thru Fridays. We had field trips, hikes up at Tantalus, swim classes at San Souci Beach and the Waikiki Natatorium. We went to the Waikiki Aquarium, went on picnics to other beaches, to Bishop Museum just to name a few places. A special Parks & Recreation Bus would take us to these places and on our way home we would all sing, P-A-P-A-K-O-L-E-A stands for PAPAKOLEA. My childhood was very nice without any bullying and everyone having fun with each other. All the kids learned and played volleyball with the adults. I became a great volleyball player and being short, I became an ace server and set up person. I am not kidding, for a kid, I was darn good!!! All the kids were good!!! Usually, we played with 3 kids and 3 adults on a team. The adults had no mercy on us. You better play to win, and they would spike the ball on you, and you had to be sure you could pick it up and move in the air!!! When I was in the 6th Grade, I was asked to teach my classmates hula routines for our May Day Program. I was always interested in sharing & teaching my friends to dance.

From the 7th Grade, I continued to teach my friends as I was really preparing myself for my secret desire to become an entertainer. My family were all either musicians or dancers and I was always asked to entertain at a lot of luaus, pageants, school functions, and on the floats in the parades. It was natural for me to entertain as I loved it so much and did it most of my life.

My parents taught me that being an entertainer was great; however, I had to be educated in another career as entertaining was just temporary and I needed to back that up with something more permanent that I could depend on for a life career.

Leilehua High School

During the summer before I went into the 9th grade, my Dad got promoted to be a District Manager for Hawaiian Telephone Company and we moved to Wahiawa which was considered the country and my first friend that I made there was Maxine K. We met at a movie matinee as both of us were by ourselves. Maxine was always there for me whenever I wanted her to spend the night with me and hang out, she would always come over. She was like a BFF and big sister to me. Maxine and I have been best friends in high school and are still good friends today. She lives in California and I live in Florida. I used to teach my friends to dance hula & we would bake cookies & sell them to our friends & neighbors to make money for our costumes. I played the piano and sang also and taught my girlfriends how to harmonize and sing at our school functions. We were very good especially harmonizing "Sweet Someone".

My friends, Gloria, Winona, Kuzing & Pat C. entertained at St. Stephen's Episcopal Church Luau on June 11, 1955, Kamehameha Day, which is a legal Hawaiian Holiday. My Dad's cuz, Mahi Beamer and Genoa Keawe and her Group including my Dad's Brother, Uncle Alika, the Steel Guitar Player also entertained. It was a Church Building Fund and tickets were sold for $3.00 for adults and $1.00 for children.

When I was in the 10th Grade, I was selected to be on Leilehua's May Day Court representing the Princess of Niihau and wore a white, satin, wrap sarong (kikepa) with Shell Leis.

My girlfriends were all majorettes and marched at the football games half-time and every Monday for the ROTC Parades. I fell in love with their white boots with tassels and wanted to be a majorette too!!! My friend, Ilima, gave me her old pair of majorette boots and I loved wearing them then my friends encouraged me to try out for the corp. I did and was selected to be a majorette!!!

When I was in the 11th grade, a classmate of mine who was also a popular football player, Gaylen L., asked me to be his campaign manager as he was running for our Class President. I asked him what my duties were and he said, we had to make posters and we also made cardboard ribbons which said, "Larsen for President". I even made up a hula and danced the hula named "Larsen for President" and he won!!! Whoo Hoo!!! We became good friends, and he took me to my Junior Prom even though I moved to Haleiwa and transferred to Waialua High School.

One of the mischievous situations I remember while I attended Leilehua was when my majorette girlfriends (Marilyn, Gwen, Winona, Loretta, Kuzing, Pat) and I decided to cut out of school (played hooky) and went to the reservoir to just hang out and swim in our bra & panties. At school at 10 am every morning, the absenteeism list was posted & everyone knew that we all hung out together, so they knew we all were not sick at the same time. Since I had the best penmanship, my girlfriends convinced me to write their excuse notes for the following day. It would have worked except I had a class with the Vice-Principal, Mr. Betsui, as my instructor in Audio Visual and he recognized my writing. Busted!!!

Mr. Betsui called all of us in his office and gave us detention for 2 hours for 2 days after school and 2 Saturdays for 2 hours each day to pull weeds on the school grounds. We were lucky that he didn't call our parents to tell them about us playing hooky. Our fathers all had prominent jobs like a Police Officer, Head of Security, General Director of the Telephone Company, etc. Detention after school was fine except for one Saturday that got me in trouble with my parents. I normally took hula lessons at Hale Koa (a building where we had recreation activities) on Saturday afternoon and that Saturday my parents went there to tell me that they were going into Honolulu as there were no cell phones then. They couldn't find me, and it was closed!!! I was at school pulling weeds but didn't want to tell them where I was. I always think of the results of my actions before I make a decision. I knew that if I told them what happened and me playing hooky at school and the results of my detention, it would affect my future. By this I mean, I wasn't afraid of the playing hooky part. I was more afraid that my parents would make me pull weeds at home every weekend for the rest of my single life and I would rather pay the consequences than confess that to them. I was put on restriction for two weeks and trust me, that was better than pulling weeds for the rest of my single life!!! Did I learn a lesson from this??? Yes, I learned never to cut out of school again especially with my close girlfriends!!! I had never told my Mom where I was that day and wish I had told her when I got married as we would have had a good laugh about it since I was an adult.

A cute story was when my Ma asked me to spell "refrigerator" as she was writing a letter to her sister. I answered r-e-f-r-i…and she said what!!! R-e-f-r-i …and I said just write "ice box" and we both laughed.

As a majorette, I loved marching at the football games and we even marched at the Shriners All Star Football Game at the end of the Football Season at Honolulu Stadium. I felt so special!!! I was a majorette for a year and 2 months in Leilehua High School then transferred to Waialua High School since my parents built a beach home at Haleiwa Beach. I tried to commute from Haleiwa to Leilehua five days a week, but it was a very long day for me as I had to leave at 6:30 am to get a ride with my Dad who worked in Wahiawa at 7:30 am. I would go to my girlfriend's, Winona, home and get a ride with her to school. School was out at 2:30 pm and I had to wait in my Dad's office from 3:00 pm to 4:30 pm to get a ride home. I did this for two months then decided to transfer to Waialua High School.

When I started going to school at Waialua, I asked if they had a majorette corp and they said no. Well, I decided to start one and trained the eight girls that were selected to be in our corp. I convinced our Home Economics instructor, Miss Seo, to be our Advisor along with the Band instructor, Mr. Onishi, and after three months of training, our majorette corp was born!!!

We marched to songs like "Don't Be Cruel" and "Rock Around the Clock" which I choreographed. We were kicking it!!! Our band played it so well; it was easy to choreograph it!!! They Rocked!!! I became very good friends with Pipi, a cheerleader. We had a lot in common especially since our parents were very strict as they were very over-protective with us, and we went everywhere together. We weren't allowed to date anyone since our parents wanted us to go to college!!! My cuz, Rosie A., was also a cheerleader for school and didn't realize we were related in high school at that time.

At the end of our football season when I was a Senior, I decided to enter a parade in Honolulu with our majorette corp. I contacted the "27th Infantry Wolfhound Regiment Army Band" at Scofield Barracks Base, Wahiawa, Oahu, and they agreed to back us in the parade. The Wolfhound Band invited the majorette corp and me to rehearse with them for an hour to the tune of "Cherry Pink & Apple Blossom White". We did a ChaCha routine to it. After rehearsing for an hour, we had lunch with the Wolfhound Band. On Saturday at the "Fiesta Hawaiiana Parade" at Ala Moana, we placed "First Place for the Marching Bands" and was presented with the trophy which we gave to our High School. We won the M.A. Blair Perpetual Sweepstakes Calabash and also a trophy for placing First in the Interscholastic Division. We competed against prominent schools in Honolulu: Roosevelt High School Majorette Corps., and also St. Louis High School Drill Team and Band. We were scheduled to march in the March of Dimes Parade, which was held on Saturday, January 19, 1957, in Honolulu. The parade was 3 miles long on Ala Moana Blvd. and we were kicking it!!! Outstanding!!! I felt so proud that we won, and I organized and trained our majorettes!!! A special mahalo to the 27th Infantry Wolfhound Regiment Army Band from Schofield Barracks, Wahiawa.

As a Senior, I decided I wanted to be a Probation Officer. I thought that would have been an interesting job. My Mom asked my Aunt, who was a Probation Officer, to enlighten me on the requirements that I needed. She took me into her office and asked me why I wanted to be a Probation Officer. She asked me, what are you going to do when you are in a room with a woman and she pulls a knife on you??? I said a

woman can pull a hidden knife on me??? At that moment, I immediately made a career change!!! I decided I would rather be a school teacher preferably for the 2nd grade.

I took the entrance exam which was very difficult for the University of Hawaii (UH) and received my acceptance letter on April 1, 1957, and wondered if it was a joke since it was April Fool's Day. After I graduated from High School, I was accepted into the University of Hawaii. I attended it for one semester then my Dad got killed in an automobile head-on collision and I decided to drop out of college & wanted to go to work.

I was not interested in going back to the University of Hawaii. I was taking courses that I felt I would not use in the future or should I say I was not interested in those courses. The main subjects were having to write out a thesis every weekend on simple things like what I did for the summer, what I planned to do next spring, etc. I was discouraged because I am not a natural writer and it took me the whole weekend to write the thesis which was due every Monday. I felt good about my thesis and then received a C grade for it!!! Really worked hard on my thesis and hated that course. I spent every weekend on it and couldn't get better than a C!!! While I was at the UH, I had no life because of that!!! Another course that I didn't like was Economics. There were also a lot of fun distractions at the UH. Hemingway Hall was a great place that had local entertainers come in and entertain us for free. Two of the entertainers were Martin Denny and his musical group and Arthur Lyman and his musical group. The UH didn't require a student to go to any of its classes. You just had to be there for the exams to pass your class. The exams covered half of the information that were lectured and the other half from our textbook. The UH is a very good college but it wasn't for me. My Mom had me talk with a very good friend of my parents, Joe Lee, Accountant Head for the Hawaiian Telephone Company, who asked me what I wanted to do next. I told him that I wanted to work for Hawaiian Tel but wanted to go to Business College first. I enjoyed my business courses there especially Business Law and Speedwriting which is similar to Shorthand. My girlfriend, Henrietta, and I went for lunch one day and was hired right off Fort Street to do typing and filing for an attorney's office which was our first job after school for three hours. I graduated from Honolulu Business College in a year and got hired by Hawaiian Telephone Company where I worked for 7 years.

In 1958, I was selected for the City of Honolulu Lei Day Royal Court as a Crown Bearer and still have the complimentary thank you letter from Mayor Neal Blaisdell.

I enjoyed working for Hawaiian Tel with my BFF, Yvonne D., who I met at the UH. We both worked at the Business Office that handled any customer service like first time installation for a residence phone, anything that required the bill, problems regarding the service, etc., and any problem that required customer service. Yvonne sat across from me; our desks were facing each other. She is such an upbeat, positive, and funny person and made my day go by very quickly. Yvonne would even go to watch me entertain during my shows. We used to go and see Don Ho with Freddie P., and Roberta D. every weekend. Would you believe, Yvonne and I got pregnant along with seven other women in our office at the same time??? The German Measles was going around that time and we all had to take that horrible, ugly shot…1 in each cheek…which was very painful!!! The needle was very long, and I almost passed out!!!

While working at Hawaiian Tel, I worked as a hula model at the Honolulu International Airport & Hilton Hawaiian Village greeting tourists and having my picture taken with them. For more details, read my Chapter on Hula Model. In 1959, I took lessons from JOHN PIILANI WATKINS, who was a Kumu Hula, choreographer, owner/manager and musician originally from Hana, Maui. John had a beautiful falsetto voice and played the piano for his Revues. Some of the songs John composed were Hana Chant, Waikaloa, Meka Nani A'u KauPo, and Ulupalakua. We would have lessons on Saturday morning and then go to the International Market Place to put on an outdoor show for the tourists at 12:00 pm.

One day I was watching the boys practice their Samoan Knife Dance and was trying to do it and John happened to see me. When the guys were performing at the show, John paged me to the stage while they were doing their knife dance and handed me a Samoan knife and that was my debut as a Woman Knife Dancer and named me, "SA, THE WOMAN SAMOAN KNIFE DANCER". Within a week I was featured doing my dance blindfolded.

I eventually got a year's contract at the Fort DeRussey Officers Club on Waikiki Beach, which is currently Hale Koa Hotel, with my hula sisters, Patty, Eulwilde, Ann, Paulette and Charlene and Samoan knife dancers George, Bully, John and Leonard and a 7-year-old hula dancer, Kathy Gore, plus 3 musicians, The Lilikoi Sisters and me. Johnny Watkins gave us his blessing and allowed all of his dancers to perform together. The Lilikoi Sisters, ages 14, 16 and 17, were recommended to me by a family member and they were outstanding!!! That was the beginning of my entertainment career as a manager, choreographer and dancer, of my first professional group,

"Carmen Souza's Polynesian Revue". I was the oldest in the group at the age of 22.

I got married in 1960 and my KUMU HULA, Johnny Piilani Watkins, brought his entire revue to perform for my wedding at Wheeler Air Force Officers Club with a 2-hour extravaganza. It was the group that performed with me and more dancers!!! Everyone couldn't stop talking about that many months after my wedding.

In October 1962, my Revue was asked to perform at the Aloha Week Hoolaulea in Waikiki. The Hoolaulea is still celebrated every year in September where the main street,

Kalakaua Ave., is blocked off for a large block party. Lots of well-known professional entertainers and dancers perform on the stages or floats. Local ono, (delicious) Plate Lunches from all nationalities are cooked and sold there. Drinks, leis, Hawaiian crafts and souvenirs are sold also. Now that is a very big deal!!! Our Polynesian Revue was fortunate to perform on two different stages: 7:00 pm in front of the International Market Place and another in front of Waikiki Liberty House at 9:00 pm on Kalakaua Avenue. I was given my choices of where we performed and also got to choose the time I wanted to perform. We received a lot of compliments and a "Certificate of Meritorious Service"

Hawaii's Annual

Aloha Week

Certificate of Meritorious Service

In grateful acknowledgement to

CARMEN SOUZA'S POLYNESIAN REVUE

HOOLAULEA

for the valuable services rendered in the promotion, and active support of, the Aloha Week project for the preservation of Hawaiian Tradition and Culture for all the Residents of these Hawaiian Islands and The Friends Who Visit Us.

October 22, 1962
DATE ISSUED

Aloha Week Hawaii, Inc.

J. Ward Russell
PRESIDENT

EXECUTIVE SECRETARY

for our performances from Hawaii's Annual Aloha Week Hawaii, Inc., signed by J. Ward Russell, President.

Heali'i's Polynesian Revue

Kathy Gore, our 7-year-old hula and Tahitian soloist Star in our revue, moved to San Diego with her family in 1967 as a Navy family. Kathy formed her own revue as Heali'i's Polynesian Revue in 1967, 53 years ago, at the age of 13 and still performs in San Diego. Before Covid-19, her Revue included 230 dancers and 20 musicians.

Kathy Heali'i's Polynesian Revue includes her Ohana (Family) which includes her daughter, Edieann Heali'i', Alaka'i (Instructor), Choreographer and Artistic Director; her sons, Anthony Kauka Stanley, Musical Director, Dancer, Drummer, and also an Endorsed Artist for Kala Ukulele and James Keolamaikalani, Male Choreographer, Alaka'i and Video Director of their revues. The beautiful sounds of Keahi Rozet, Lead Vocalist and Guitarist of "One Island the Band" and Kathy's husband, Eddie, formerly a Dancer, is their Stage Manager of her Revue. I am a large fan of families who perform together. Kathy is the Kumu Hula, Choreographer, Manager, M.C., and Director of her Revue. Whenever Covid-19 is gone and it's safe to travel, September is her big performance for the Pacific Islander Festival in San Diego. Good time to see her Revue and say hi to Kathy. Tell her Kanoe sends her aloha. For the past two years, Kathy has been the President for the Southern Kumu Association of California, Kulia Ika

Punawai, which meets quarterly. You can watch her Revue on You Tube under "Heali'i's Polynesian Revue at PIFA (Pacific Islander Festival Association) 2016, 2019 and 2020".

I am so proud of Kathy Heali'i'onalani Gore Stanley and her accomplishments!!! Kathy is also special to our family. She became Keone's, my youngest son, God-mother at the age of 13 years old.

Kathy and I were proud to be students of our Kumu Hula John Piilani Watkins. He had the most beautiful falsetto voice, played the piano, uke, and MC in all our Revues. JOHN PIILANI WATKINS was THE BEST!!!

★ Fear holds back people from living their dream!!! Always follow your dream!!! ★

John Piilani Watkins

K umu Hula John Piilani Watkins was a Composer, Recording and Musical Artist, Choreographer, Pianist, M.C., Judge at the Merrie Monarch Festival, President of Hui O Piilani, performed as John Piilani Watkins and his Heavenly Hawaiian, President of Hui O Piilani, and Kumu Hula of Halau O Piilani. He was also inducted into the Hawaiian Falsetto Music Hall of Fame on October 13, 2006, at the Aloha Festival Falsetto Contest in Waikiki. Among his popular chants and songs were Hana Chant, Waikaloa, Meka Nani Ao Kaupo, and Ulupalakua, just to name a few songs. Kathy and I both danced with his Revue and are very proud to be a product of his legacy!!! Johnny became an angel on February 25, 1983!!!

Bulgogi Beef

(Korean Bar-B-Que Teriyaki Steak)
Teriyaki or Thin Steak Strips or Thin Pork Steaks

2 green onion stalks (cut)

5 pc. diced garlic

1 cup soy sauce (Aloha Brand)

1 cup sugar

- Mix & marinate for at least 2 hour
- Fry light with olive oil
- Serve with rice and vegetables

Mahalo for sharing, Cuz Lindy from Kaneohe, Hawaii

Chinese Pretzels

1 box cornstarch

1 cup flour (sifted)

1/2 cup sugar

4 eggs, beaten

1/2 tsp. salt

1 tsp. vanilla

1 cup cream & 1 cup water or 2 cups milk

- You need a set of different designs of Rosette Irons. Google Rosette Irons and you can watch the video frying!!!
- Dip the Rosette Iron in the batter 1/4 inch from the top of the iron 375 degrees:
- Heat electric pan 3/4 full with Canola Oil
- Drain on paper towel, cool, then sprinkle powdered sugar on top!!!

Really light and so ono!!! (delicious)

3

Our Beach Home

*I*n my Junior year in High School, our family moved to our custom-built home on Haleiwa Beach which is on the North Shore of Oahu where the ocean waves would break up to our front yard. After being used to living in the mountains, the first couple of nights I slept there, I couldn't fall asleep because of the constant crashing of the waves. I gradually got used to the sound of the waves and slept like a baby. About 300 yards from our home, there was an Army Beach Pavilion owned by the U.S. Army and we were able to watch the soldiers practice life-saving maneuvers. At 10 am during the week, about 25 men would swim out past the surf and pretend they were drowning in their uniforms and another 25 men would swim out to them fully dressed in uniforms to rescue them. Whenever they were not practicing their maneuvers, the military and their families would enjoy the beach. My friends and I would swim out 200 feet to their floating dock (12' x 12') and put some half ripe mangoes in netted fruit bags between the floating barrels that held the dock together and we simply would dive down and get the mangoes and eat it whenever we got hungry. The Army Beach Pavilion had speakers blaring out all the top 50's songs which were wonderful and entertaining while we were on the dock and beach. There was also a lifeguard on duty whenever the beach was opened. Remember back then we didn't have cell phones so whenever my parents wanted me to come home, they would stand in the front yard with their hands on their hips and that was my visual signal to get my okole (butt) home.

My Dad taught me to drive our 1941 Ford (4-wheel stick shift) Army Jeep and I got my drivers' license at the age of 15. I used to drive to Waimea Falls & Waimea Bay which was only 10-15 minutes away. At Waimea Bay on Oahu's North Shore, there is a large rock that everyone loves to climb up in the ocean about 30 feet high to jump into the ocean as the waves came in. One day I was on Jump Rock and our Shop Teacher, David Akana, was there and dared me to jump from the Rock. I had never done that, and he offered to give me a $1.00 bill and I said okay but I had to take my watch off. I wasn't wearing a bathing suit, so I did the jump wearing my turquoise shorts and turquoise and white top and I did it!!! From that day forward, I always jumped from the Rock as if it was a piece of cake after breaking the ice.

Tsunami Hits Haleiwa Beach

In 1956, our family survived the horrible experience of a Tsunami. It was a Saturday morning and my Mom who was at work called my Dad to wake us up to tell us there was a tidal wave heading towards our beach home at Haleiwa. I remember my Dad telling me to pack some clothes and, of course, I grabbed my prom dresses. At that age, that was important to me. I did grab other clothes including my gowns. There was this high excitement for everyone on the Island.

The neighbors and the police were going door to door to let everyone know that the Tsunami was heading towards our beach and we needed to evacuate soon as it was estimated to hit at 11:00 am. The weather was very weird!!! It was nice and sunny but then the ocean turned a beautiful, deep blue as if someone had poured a rich blue color like bluing into the ocean. It was the color of the deep ocean whenever you are out to sea. The waves got larger and then something very weird happened!!! The water started to recede!!! It looked like someone had pulled the plug (stopper) out of the ocean and the water drained out for miles. All the coral rock and large fish were exposed. Some local guys who were lifeguards at the Army Beach ran out to grab the fish. The police told everyone we had to leave and evacuate now and head for higher ground away from the area. This was our final warning to evacuate the area.

Tidal waves hit in a set of 3's. It doesn't come on to land like a large wave that you normally see. It comes quickly into shore like it is filling up the tub or beach front and arrives so fast with such a great tremendous force that it comes in then immediately recedes out to sea again sucking and taking everything in its path that is not permanently tied down. After the third tidal wave, we got an all clear from the Police and was allowed to return to our homes to evaluate any damage.

My bamboo purse was found 500 feet from our beach home at Chun's Store and my double bed including the box springs and mattress were found 150 feet in our friends' front yard. Our living room furniture was swept out to sea and never to be found. Our kitchen appliances were ruined from the salt water and we were lucky that the owner of the appliance store came over to wash down the appliances with water and we were able to save them from the salt-water damage.

Those that I mentioned were only some of the large items. All the other smaller things were gone too. My parents asked the Red Cross for assistance and they refused to help us. My parents asked if they could help us get an interest-free loan and their answer was... "you have three cars, sell one of them". One car didn't even belong to us. It was a company car, and we needed the other two cars as both parents worked. My parents just had our beach home built and just needed a loan to fix the damage. The entire front of our beach home was open, and the contents were all gone. Needless to say, because of the Red Cross's attitude, our Ohana (family) stopped contributing to the Red Cross. This affected my other relatives and friends who also stopped giving to the Red Cross. Our home was built only 9 months before the tidal wave destroyed it!!! We lived with one of our neighbors for about six months while our home was being rebuilt.

★ *Beware of companies that make you sign an assignment of benefits (AOB) for repairs. These contractors charge double or triple of what your insurance company has estimated, and you will be responsible to pay the difference.* ★

Cold Spaghetti Salad

16 oz. pkg. spaghetti (1 lb)

4 tomatoes, chopped

1 green pepper, chopped

1 round sweet onion, chopped

8 oz.bottle Seven Seas Viva Salad Dressing

1/2 bottle McCormick Salad Supreme Seasoning (2.62 oz. bottle)

- Break spaghetti into thirds and cook.
- Add remaining ingredients.
- Serve warm or cold.

Enjoy!!!

4

Kalaupapa, Molokai

Kalaupapa, Molokai, is located on the Kalaupapa Peninsula at the base of some of the highest cliffs in the world. The cliffs rose 2,000 feet above the Pacific Ocean. In the 1870s, a leper colony was established there as a community. In 1873, Hansen's disease was caused by a bacterium which has been curable since 1940 with the use of antibiotics. The severe cases had to be quarantined on this island in the hope of preventing contagious treatment of the disease. The movie, "The Hawaiians", features the leper colony and how the people were sent there.

When I was 22, my Polynesian Dancers and I entertained at Kalaupapa. No one was allowed to go there except by invitation. There are only 3 ways to get there: private plane, boat or by an escorted mule train more than a 3-mile mountain trail which is 1,600 feet to the sea if you slipped and fell. This is the famous place where Father Damian went to live so he could help treat the Lepers then eventually contracted Leprosy himself where he died.

My dancers included Paulette, Patty, Euwilde and Ann. My good friend, Calvin M., who worked with me at an Insurance Company, also accompanied us to help us with our equipment.

We flew in on Friday afternoon via private plane and left Sunday afternoon. Our main musicians were Aunty Phil and Uncle Joe. We went there to entertain the Lepers, their Staff and also the U.S. Coast Guard that were stationed there, for New Years' Eve. We stayed at the hospital. It was quite interesting, and I was surprised to learn that the pilot was my Uncle Herman B., married to my Mom's cousin. We were not allowed to mingle with the Lepers that were infected. We were escorted around the town by the people that were cured but decided to live there as this is the only home they had known for most of their lives. Only the very badly infected Lepers were sent there, and they had their own town consisting of stores, a hospital, etc. We went on a tour the next day and visited Father Damian's Gravesite and St. Philomena Church which had holes in the floor in front of the pews so the patients with excessive drool would spit through the holes to the ground during the church service. We were told Father Damian was being considered for being canonized as a Saint which was finalized in 2009. Father Damian went there to help the Lepers and he ended up with leprosy and passed there. There were other stores which we were not allowed to visit.

The town had nice homes for the patients which were rented for only $120.00 a month. Only adults lived there. If a couple got pregnant, the baby was removed as soon as its birth and flown to the relatives in Honolulu for fear of contracting the Leper disease for the baby's protection. The only people allowed to live there besides the patients were the doctors, nurses, admin staff, cooks and the U.S. Coast Guard. Everything was close and you didn't need a car. I remember a Chinese Gentleman that had a Cadillac which he proudly drove around town.

A cone shaped island was pointed out where early sea captains, with boatloads of new patients, would anchor there forcing frightened Leper passengers to jump overboard and swim for Kalaupapa shore in the cold, rough ocean. One of the things that impressed me were the "opihis", which was the size of a 3-4" pancake, which were very tasty, juicy and very tender. An opihi is an island delicacy…a matured barnacle or a mollusk… basically scraped off the rocks with a screwdriver or spoon as the waves receded. Back In 1960, these mollusk delicacies were sold for $40.00 for a gallon in Honolulu measuring only 1-1/2 inches and today it is very expensive, $60.00 a pound or $250 per gallon. Expensive but worth it!!!

When it was time to entertain, a large gymnasium was decorated for us to put on our Revue. There was an invisible line which divided the basketball court that we weren't allowed to cross. The staff, any workers, the Coast Guard and the entertainers were on one side and the Lepers were on the other side. We had to dance with tabis, the Japanese white cloth footwear, which was mandatory and wore them all the time we were there for our protection. When we left, we had to dispose of them which were burned in fire. No one knew what caused Leprosy also known as Hansen's Disease, so we weren't allowed to take anything when we flew out. We received tabis as soon as we arrived and wore them everywhere.

Today Kalaupapa is a designated Kalaupapa National Historical Park. Only 100 outside visitors are allowed into the park each day. Visitors must have permits and cannot talk to the former patients, take their photos or enter their properties. No one under age 16 is allowed to visit there.

We felt very special to be asked to perform at Kalaupapa as it was by invitation only and not opened to the public.

Chinese Almond Cookies

3 cups flour

1 1/4 cups sugar

2 tsp. baking soda

1 cup Crisco & 1 block butter

- Add (1) egg & (1) tsp. almond extract & mix well
- Roll into small balls (a quarter or 25 cents size)
- Place on ungreased cookie sheet & press center with red food coloring
- I use the other end of a wooden spoon with cotton to make this impression
- Bake 15 min. at 350 degrees

Makes 10 dozen

Really ono!!!

5

Hula Model

$\mathcal{I}$ became a part-time hula model that greeted tourists at Honolulu International Airport three times a week and also greeted movie stars and entertainers as Sidney Poitier and Ringo Starr which were featured in Movie Magazines and also with Wayne Newton, Les Crane, the Ice Capades Stars of 1964 and the Four Amigos.

Two of the most memorable pictures were taken with Ringo Starr, the Beatles, and Academy Award Movie Star, Sidney Poitier. I was featured in the following magazines with Ringo in Teen-ville Magazine, featuring the Beatles on the cover, November 1964; Screen Life Magazine, January 1965 featuring Steve McQueen & Paul Newman on the cover; Movie TV Secrets featuring Jackie Kennedy on the cover, November 1964 all sold for 35 cents each.

Kammy and I were working at the Honolulu International Airport that night at the Domestic Arrivals when our Photographer came up to us and said we have to greet Ringo Starr at the International Terminal. This was very unusual for us as we only worked at the Domestic Arrivals. When we got

there, we were introduced to Ringo, and had our pictures taken with him. The next morning our picture with Ringo appeared on the front page of a San Francisco newspaper, which was taken by the United Press International (UPI) with the caption, "Ringo's Reception". Beatles drummer Ringo Starr, draped in leis, paused to pose with hula girls, Carmen Souza and Magnolia M. in Honolulu en route to rejoining his group in Australia after an enthusiastic reception

in San Francisco. It was an exciting night, and we felt very special to have our picture taken with Ringo!!! My brothers, Keoki, Kimo and Mel, who lived in Santa Clara, California, called me to tell me about Ringo's picture and they were so excited and wanted to know how I happened to have my picture taken with him. They were teens and a Beatles fan & would always tell their friends that their sister was the person in the picture with Ringo!!! Whenever I went to visit them, they would always introduce me to their friends as the sister that took a picture with Ringo. All their friends were very impressed and made me feel very special!!!

Another evening my Photographer, Darryl, took us over to the International Arrivals. When we got there, he told me that we were greeting Sidney Poitier during a stop-over on his Tokyo-bound trip for the opening of his Oscar winning film, *Lilies of the Field*. Sidney Poitier and I were in the Honolulu Advertiser/Star Bulletin the next morning and the Movie Life Magazine, February 1965, with Ann Margaret on the cover (25 cents) and United Airlines Mainliner, June 1965. I have an original magazine of each of these. I was on a flight home from San Francisco and was looking thru the United Mainliner and saw my picture in it with Sidney and the flight attendants gave me five issues for souvenirs.

I was also a Hula Model at the Hilton Hawaiian Village Luaus once a week. It was interesting how I found out I was in those movie magazines. I was working at Hawaiian Telephone Company and returned from lunch one day and several of my co-workers told me that they saw my picture in the movie magazines. Of course, I rushed out to get a copy of it and still have the original magazines.

I met my best friend, Freddie P., when I worked at the airport as a Hula Model. He was a lei greeter for the Hawaii Visitors Bureau, and we got to be great friends to hang out with. I had to do a commercial for Chevrolet at the airport with a football team and didn't want to go there by myself at 4:30 am when the flight was due, so Freddie went with me. We also went clubbing together with our other girlfriends. I remember one incident when I was supposed to meet Freddie and was driving to meet him. Well, my gas gauge was not accurate and as I drove along the Ala Wai Canal, my car started to cough or hiccup. Well, I had never run out of gas before and it finally stopped in the middle of Ala Wai Blvd. I saw a jogger go by and asked him if he could help me push my car to the side of the street. He said okay but he had to finish his run which was about 50 feet away. I waited and he helped me and advised me that I had run out of gas.

What??? That had never happened to me!!! I thanked him for helping me. Picture this!!! Cell phones did not exist at that time so I had to run to meet Freddie before he would think that I was a no show. It was 15 minutes away and I ran as fast as I could. That was when I was younger and had a lot of energy!!! Thank, God, Freddie waited for me & we went to get gas for my car. Well, it's a good thing he knew how to start my car. It took two of us. I had to start the car & he had to do something to the carburetor to get the car started. I thought I only had to put gas in the tank. Whew!!! I learned my life lesson and don't trust the gas gauge anymore and always fill my car before it gets to the 1/4 tank mark.

Freddie and I used to go dancing at the Merrie Monarch and the Peppermint Lounge with 8 of our girlfriends. He was the only guy in our group, and he looked like he could be our pimp as all the girls were very attractive. We would all sit at one large table and all the men would ask us to dance.

Freddie and I went to the beach one day with Wayne Newton, his brother, George and Wayne Newton's girlfriend, a Japanese Singer at the Hilton Hawaiian Village. Sorry, I don't remember her name, but she was a headliner at the Hilton at that time. We went with our friends, Glen Smith, and the band from Canada who performed at the Peppermint Lounge, who were good friends with Wayne Newton. We had a nice time at the beach!!!

My best friends, Freddie, Yvonne D., Roberta D. and I always went to see Don Ho at Duke Kahanamoku's at the International Market Place every weekend where a lot of the local entertainers went to jam after they finished playing at their hotels and clubs. Popular entertainers I remember were Kui Lee, composer of "I'll Remember You"; Sonny Chillingsworth, great guitarist and singer; Danny Kaleikini, beautiful soloist singer headliner at the Hilton Hawaiian Village; the Among Brothers and the Alii's. Don Ho used to call me on stage to dance "San Francisco" whenever he sang it. All the hula dancers and musicians from the other hotels would dance on stage too. Duke's was like a meeting place after work to have fun and just unwind and jam with friends.

Getting thirsty and need to take a LUA Break!!! It's shee, shee (pee) time!!! Hey, going to start making Chicken Long Rice. It's easy and very ono!!! Hope you enjoy it!!!

Chicken Long Rice

2 lbs. skinless chicken thighs and drumsticks rub Hawaiian salt or rock salt to taste

3 pkg (10.5 oz. pink pkg) long rice noodles. (Buy at Dong-A, Mills Ave. north of 50 in Orlando, FL)

2 garlic cloves (minced or crushed)

2 Tb. fresh minced ginger, 2 Tb. vegetable oil

12 cups of water w/ "Knorr Chicken Flavor Granules Bouillon" for Broth (1/2 tsp. to 1 cup boiling water)

- Cut chicken into small pieces & brown chicken
- Saute garlic & ginger with the chicken
- Gradually add 4 cups of broth & bring to boil on medium heat. Add the rest of the broth as needed.
- Cook until the chicken is tender....1 1/2 hour
- Soak the long rice for the last 30 min. before you add to broth. Cut into smaller pieces & add to chicken & broth.
- Cook for another 5-10 minutes & garnish with chopped green onions.

6

My First Wish: Guam, USA

*I*n 1969, our family was sent to the island of Guam since my husband was in the Navy. I got a job as a Secretary for a Commander with the Naval Communications Station (NCS) and got a promotion from a GS-3 (clerical assistant) to a GS-4 (secretary) when I moved from California to Guam. When we arrived in 1969, we all discovered how different life was. There was only one TV station and it was only in black and white, can you imagine, that operated from 3:00 pm to 8:00 pm, and only one radio station which was operated by the Andersen Air Force Base with the news and all types of music. I believe in the year 1972, cable TV finally came to Guam in "Living Color" and that was a real treat!!! In November 1969, I started to work at the Naval Communication Station (N.C.S.) as a secretary to a Commander in the Navy.

I worked in a building that handled all the Naval Communications in the Pacific and Micronesia. Everyone had to be cleared as Top Secret or Secret; military and civil service workers. We had 700 navy men, 12 marines who checked our IDs before we entered the building and 12 women!!! I was the Secretary to the Commander and besides secretarial duties, I used to be a proof-reader of any documents or correspondence that the Commander received. If my initials were not on any correspondence, the Commander wouldn't read it until I read it and initialed it.

I used to wear mini dresses and skirts to work and the men would tell me, if they would drop a dollar on the floor, would I pick it up??? I said of course!!! Dirty young navy men put ten dimes on the floor 10 inches apart. I was smart, I didn't bend over to pick it up, I just bent my knees and picked it up!!! Those were my younger days when I was flexible!!!

I was late for work one morning and was pulled over by a police officer by the side of the road who had pulled over a school bus. I went into the middle turning lane to pass him and he flagged me to pull over and said that I couldn't drive in that lane unless I was going to turn left, and he still gave me a ticket for $55.00. When I got to work, my Navy Commander told me that I wouldn't win when I insisted, I was going to fight my case. No one wins in their court. I went to court and explained to the Judge that I was going to make a left turn and had pictures taken by my husband, Chuck, naval photographer, and little model cars to illustrate this and won my case. The best part was to have the court refund me with a check for $55.00 to show my Commander and which I framed and kept at work on my desk!!! About six months later, I was entertaining at the Cliff Hotel and this officer came into the club. I went up to him and said, "Do you remember me???" He said yes. He asked me if I was really going to make a left turn. I looked at him and smiled and winked and said, "I could have" as I walked away with a sassy sway!!!

I worked at NCS for about a year and six months then left my position for a promotion to work for the Catholic and Protestant Navy Chaplains. My duties were different: Taking appointments for the military families for counseling for getting married, religious, and personal things; accounting, going to the bank and whatever needed to be done. The Protestant Chaplain tried to get me to walk his dog and I asked the Catholic Chaplain if that was one of my duties and he said "Hell, no!!!" Thank, God!!! I got all my work done by 8:30 am then had to do paperwork and greet the military and their dependents the rest of the day. It wasn't long before I exhausted everything I could do for the Chaplains, I asked permission to bring and hand sew my accessories for my beautiful Polynesian costumes which kept me busy in between my assigned duties to greet the military personnel. I worked there for a year then resigned to entertain full-time.

While I was working there, my car was due for a safety inspection with the Guam Transportation to renew my registration for another year. Chuck was supposed to take the car in, but he was on a flight assignment taking pictures and he and the guys crashed on Pagan Island. I received a call that he and the other guys were fine and couldn't be rescued for a couple of days. I was not happy about him being stranded because I didn't want to take the car in for the safety check. The word was it was not easy to pass the inspection and to make sure the men took the car in. Well, I went home and got a care bag ready to be dropped on the island for Chuck and put things in it for him and wrote an unhappy note on a roll of toilet paper. Chuck said he was the most popular guy with the only roll of toilet paper!!! I took the car in and put on my cutest mini skirt outfit with a low plunging neckline and I passed the safety inspection!!! Whew!!!

The Movie, *Noon Sunday*

My daughters, Michelle and Mataiva, were selected to be in a movie called *Noon Sunday*. It featured MARK LENARD, JOHN RUSSELL AND LOVELY LINDA AVERY. It's about two assassins, saboteurs, on a desperate dangerous mission, fighting for freedom. Two guerrilla leaders must be stopped before a missile site can be established… a power station must be demolished as a diversion…and a double agent must be eliminated. It's an impossible mission with no second chances. Filmed on location in the steamy Pacific, it's a sizzling action-adventure with an explosive mix of intrigue and danger…the suspense ticks-away like a time bomb toward *Noon Sunday*, a deadline for death!!! My daughters with five other children had to march into the church with the Nuns singing "Onward Christian Soldiers". While the children were in the church, the ticking bomb explodes and kills everyone. The heroes catch the guerrilla leaders. March 27, 1971, was the Premiere for this movie and Michelle presented the Governor's wife and First Lady with a bouquet of two dozen red roses!!!

Meeting the Local People
& Joining the Volleyball Women's Team

On a beautiful island, when things really got slow, I would find other things to occupy my time. I signed up to play volleyball with the local Guamanian residents from Barrigada Village. On the island of Guam, the native language is called "Chamorro" (Cha mor' ro). I was the only player on the team that didn't speak Chamorro so whenever the coach, who was also the Mayor of Barrigada Village, would brief the players or we would get in a huddle, I would have to remind him to please translate in English what you just told the team??? It so happened on this Guamanian Girls' Volleyball Team, I was one of the shortest players but made first string; however, I made up the difference as being one of the best volleyball setters and servers for our team. After the games, the coach would take our team to McDonalds to eat which was always a treat for us. Our family was invited to go to all their Village Festivals which consisted of the local food and music and became good friends with the local families. We even got our coach's sister, Emma, to work and live with us and care for our son, Keone, age one, after school and help care for our other children, Michelle and Mataiva. Emma was part of our family and even had her own Military ID Card and we all loved her!!!

My God given gift to dance, teach, educate and love to entertain kept calling to me…dancers will understand this feeling… so I decided to start a Polynesian Group. I wrote an article for our Navy Paper and asked for anyone that could dance, sing, or play an instrument to contact me. I received a lot of responses and most of the drummers were all haole (Caucasian), one Guamanian guy and two Hawaiians, all military men and one was a Polynesian Fire Knife Dancer. I selected and trained the dancers who were all Guamanian girls and haole girls who never danced before. After training the girls for about four months, 3 times a week for 2 hours or more, we entered a talent contest and competed with 12 other dance groups for Guam's Liberation Day on July 17th and won a trophy for "The Best Entertainment - 1970 Liberation Day." All our hard work paid off for my group of seven dancers and 5 drummers and one Samoan Fire Knife Dancer. After winning the Best Entertainment Trophy, we started getting more gigs to entertain for various restaurants and night clubs.

We got our lucky break while entertaining at an Air Force Luau for the singer of our group, Sandy, and impressed a very popular columnist, Joe Murphy, who used to include our group in his column, Pipe Dreams, which got us free publicity and had the locals and tourists coming to watch us perform at different clubs and restaurants. Our first paid gig was at the Pirates Cove every Sunday afternoon and also at the Viking Room Night Club on Friday evenings.

One of my dancers, Anita, told me that the Cliff Hotel was looking for a Polynesian Group. I told her to get me more information and a phone number and I would contact the Owner and President Bob Jones. Currently, the Cliff Hotel was the elite and classiest hotel in Guam that was on a mountain side that overlooked the city.

We were performing at the Viking Room at 10:00 pm and
Anita gave me Bob Jones's home phone number about 8:30
pm when we checked in for our performance. I immediately
called him by phone (there were no cell phones in those days)
and introduced myself saying "This is Kanoe, from Kanoe's
Polynesian Revue" and said that I heard you are looking
for a Polynesian Group to perform for your hotel. You are

welcome to view our Revue and we were performing at 10:00 pm. He said it was too late, but he made me an offer I could not refuse. Apparently, our reputation preceded us, and he had been reading a lot of very positive and very nice comments regarding our group and was very aware of our reputation. Bob told me he was having about 300 Japanese Tourists fly in from Japan for a weekend in Saipan, an island about 45 minutes from Guam by Air Micronesia. He flew us

to Saipan, put us in his other hotel, The Royal Taga Hotel, and covered our meals and expenses.

We were scheduled to put on two revues for 45-minutes each, one on Friday evening and one on Saturday evening. My group was hired to perform on site unseen. Bob Jones had never seen our revue but went strictly by our reputation. We performed our revue on Friday evening, and I had a brief meeting with Bob Jones when it was over and asked him what his thoughts were, and he replied, "You're hired!!!" We were so excited as we were going to entertain the Japanese Tourists three times a week at a luau at their private beach property. Bob requested that we change our name from Polynesian Revue to Micronesian Revue as Guam was competing with Hawaii for the tourists. We experienced three wonderful and exciting years on the beach for luaus then relocated the luaus to the Cliff Hotel and also started to perform at the Cliff Hotel Red Carpet Night Club on Saturday evenings accompanied by Ricky and the Donderos, a seven-member band from the Philippines. So in between our dances, the Donderos performed their own variety show and did imitations of famous singers, jokes and also featured their own band with their songs during our costume changes.

The hotels started to build up around Tumon Bay: Guam Hilton Hotel, the Guam Tokyu Hotel and the Guam Dai Ichi Hotel. Our Micronesian Revue became so well-known that whenever the Polynesian Groups went on vacation for two weeks, we were hired to perform at those hotels. All the entertainers would come to our show and hang out with us after their shows as the Cliff Hotel became a Disco Night Club after our show.

My First Wish: Japan

In April 1972, we were rehearsing at my home and the General Manager, Tony Oishi from the Guam Tokyu Hotel, called me and asked me if we wanted to go to Japan to entertain. I said sure but what about your group. He said they couldn't go because he needed them to entertain at his hotel. That weekend, Tony O., brought the Japanese Management Team from Japan to watch our Revue. As soon as our show was done, we all sat down and they started to negotiate a contract for us to entertain for six months, five

days on and two days off a week. I told them we were not able to do that because three of our entertainers were in high school and had to be back at the end of summer. We agreed on three months, June-August 1972, with seven days on and no days off.

Our special team in our Micronesian Revue were: Barb D., Marie B., Rhonda L., Delfin D., & Joey F. We were hired to entertain at Hotel Juraku, Iizaka-Spa, which is Prefecture to Fukushima. I would describe it like Orlando having different counties. The last big tidal wave in Fukushima, Japan, was about an hour away. We had to fly into Tokyo, Japan, then get on a train about three hours from there. We had to be quick because the train just stopped for five minutes and we had about 30 bags and had to board that train during the 5-minute stop because the doors of the train closed and left. The hotel sent us our interpreter and guide, HISA, and men to help with our luggage and we all knew we had to move very quickly!!! We arrived at the hotel and was greeted like real celebrities. The entire hotel staff were lined up outside to bow and greet us with great respect!!!

This was a resort spa for Japanese companies who transported their male employees there for rest and recreation for two nights. There were no female guests. This is a first-class resort with a great Japanese atmosphere. It was very nice to be surrounded by the Japanese and learn about their culture and way of being entertained and respected which is different from the American way. In my opinion, it wasn't about title, salary or status. This was for everyone and to show how much they are appreciated.

This hotel had a very large indoor, hot heated spa and pool for men, larger than a swimming pool which is 50 x 100. We gals got to use the women's spa and pool and it was like heaven!!! No one spoke English and we were assigned an English-Speaking Interpreter, HISA. It was funny sometimes when we thought he understood us and he didn't. A lot of foreigners who cannot understand English can read it and understand it.

Two days before our contract began, the entire show had a dress rehearsal. At that time, the management was going to charge a 100 yen cover charge but after our dress rehearsal, the cover charge was increased to 300 yen. During our rehearsal, we would take a break to have sushi, hot tea and other light appetizers which we loved!!! The Japanese House Band backed our show with our two musicians and singers, Del and Joey. I had our music arrangements for the revue so the band could read it by notes and play our entire show.

We were scheduled to entertain for 45 minutes as the Headline Main Room Entertainers. The Japanese entertainers proceeded our show then we were introduced as the featured Entertainers from Guam. We were treated like Las Vegas Main Show Entertainers. Two hours later we put on a 20-minute show in the Starlite Lounge. We put on a pool show once a week at 6:00 pm starting in July. We were paid on the 15th with Japanese yen and on the 30th with US Dollars. The object was so we would spend our yen there. At the end of our contract, we changed our yen back to US Dollars.

Let the Entertainment Begin!!!

We had a 3-bedroom dormitory apartment. The two guys, Del and Joey, had the room with 2 single beds next to the kitchen. The girls, Marie and Rhonda and Barb and I used the other bedrooms and slept on futons which were on Japanese (tatami) mats and the room decorated Japanese style. We had a pretty large kitchen and had to cook our own breakfast. The hotel supplied whatever we wanted for breakfast as eggs, ham, potatoes, bacon, milk, tea, coffee, orange juice, etc., or anything else we requested.

Lunch was eaten in any of the restaurants of our choice and we usually ate in the Soba Noodle Restaurant or the Sushi Restaurant. If we decided to go out during the day like to shop, sightseeing or to the park, the hotel would make us a Bento Box (sushi, meat, noodles, rice, fruit and a drink) to take with us. For dinner, our main course consisted of either steak, pork chops, or chicken with rice, vegetables and a dessert which was brought to our dorm every night by 5:00 pm. I forgot to negotiate our drinks in our contract. The General Manager loved me dancing the Samoan Knife Dance with a blindfold so I mentioned that I wasn't feeling too well and maybe would not be able to do my knife dance which was our main featured dance. The General Manager asked what could he do to make me feel better. I told them I wanted 2 cases of Pepsi per week and he agreed, and I was always ready to do the Knife Dance.

We only had one bathroom with a tub/shower, a toilet and a weird lavatory (sink) to brush our teeth and wash our hands and face. It looked like a spitting bowl that we use at the dentist office. We were having lunch one afternoon and I mentioned how weird it was to see toothpaste in the toilet after we flushed it. The guys laughed and said that the water came from the bowl we spit in and we all laughed about it!!! The Japanese were smart and knew how to recycle water and reuse it. The water went from the spitting bowl to the toilet tank and then used whenever it was flushed!!! How clever!!!

We used to have a problem of who was going to use the shower next, so I came up with a system. The first person waking up after 6:00 am would rush and grab a tag with a number on it. Six people, six numbers on a large hotel tag. If you had to use the toilet in between the numbers, that was a priority!!! So, after #1 was done showering, that person would call #2. Some of us would grab a # and then go back to sleep.

Our contract also included three round trip tickets for my husband, Chuck, to help move us to Japan, during July to bring us anything we needed and also so that my family could come and visit me and the last trip to help us move back to Guam at the end of our contract. We were treated very well and enjoyed entertaining there.

Every Saturday during July and two weeks of August, we met and bowled with the hotel guests and local residents. Each of us would be on a bowling lane and we weren't bowling against each other as teams, we would just bowl for the highest individual points. We would bowl for prizes such as cameras, watermelons, and different prizes and trophies. It was fun for everyone. The customers and hotel guests were bowling with the celebrities or entertainers of the revue. An interesting thing about bowling. I was a terrible bowler in the US. I asked the Assistant Manager to teach us how to bowl and he taught all of us. The lanes in Japan are the opposite of our lanes in the US. The lanes were drier. So, I used the House bowling ball which had a couple of nicks on it and rolled rough and I bowled over 260 each time. I was just as surprised as everyone else. The manager said are you sure you don't know how to bowl, and I said I'm learning…honest!!! I even got a trophy for High Series!!!

We left at the end of August to return to Guam with about 30 pieces of luggage, costumes, etc. We had to literally throw our bags, luggage, footlocker, and boxes on the train that just stopped for five minutes. We moved fast and got it done!!! At the airport, Japan Air Lines tried to charge us for excess luggage of $400.00 but after I negotiated with them, we were only charged $120.00 which was covered in our contract!!!

December 1972, The Guam Dai Ichi Hotel's group from Hawaii had two weeks off and we were hired to do our Micronesian Revue there six nights a week. I have a wonderful letter of recommendation from the Japanese Managers from Guam Transportation Company about our beautiful and outstanding performances.

In February 1973, I was a principal hula dancer four nights a week for the "Na Keiki O Polynesia Revue". at the Guam Hilton Hotel & met the Kawana Family from New Zealand that was the next group to perform. I taught the Kawana Family some hulas and they taught me their authentic Maori dances. I was performing with my Micronesian Revue in addition to this. In March 1973, seven months after we returned from Japan, the Guam Visitors Bureau asked our group to represent Guam at the P.A.T.A. (Pacific Area Travel Association) Conference for five days in Tokyo, Japan. Pan American Airlines flew us there and back. We were treated like celebrities!!! That was a big honor to represent Guam Visitors Bureau and we were also featured as "The First and Only Local Group from Guam" to entertain internationally or anywhere else. We returned to the Cliff Hotel to entertain the Japanese tourists three times a week and entertained in the Red Carpet Restaurant & Night Club every Saturday evening. Our band was Ricky and the Donderos, a seven-piece band from the Philippines who were outstanding musicians, singers & comedians.

In September and October 1973, Pan American's Director, Guam and the Trust Territories, Jim Barton, asked me if we would do a promotion for Pan Am's flights from Guam to Japan. We performed at Guam International Airport for 20 minutes before Pan Am's flight to Tokyo for four weeks. He asked me to give him a quote for five entertainers. We negotiated for 8 round trip tickets to Tokyo, Japan. After four weeks, Jim Barton asked me if we wanted to do another four-week promotion. This time we got 8 round trip tickets from Guam to Honolulu, Hawaii. On the last night of the promotion, we boarded the flight and entertained during the flight to Hawaii. We flew over together and returned whenever we wanted to separately. What a deal!!! While I was entertaining one evening at the airport, I got a phone call from the General Manager of the Guam Continental Hotel, Wilfred Hagen. He asked me if I could work for him for two weeks as his part-time secretary. I asked him what happened

CLIFF HOTEL

Nite Club Opens
9:00 - 1:00 am
NO COVER CHARGE

Come and See--Guam's Very Own!

Who are representing Guam at the Pata Conference in Tokyo

from February 26 to March 1.

SHOWTIME 10:30 pm

KANOELEHUA'S

Micronesian Revue

to his secretary. He said she was sick and would be out for two weeks. I agreed and when he asked me how much I expected as pay I said, I didn't want to get paid. I just wanted

to stay in his Japanese themed bungalow on the beach with my husband for 2 nights including our meals.

I don't normally do this; however, Wilfred was my former boss at the Cliff Hotel Night Club and I also taught his daughters to dance the hula. Our family became friends with his family. There was one problem before I could do this. I didn't have a babysitter for my children, Mataiva and Michelle. He said "no problem" my daughters, Dominique and Karen, will babysit your children. Boy, what a deal for them!!! They ate breakfast and lunch in the restaurant and played on the beach and hotel grounds and in the swimming pool while I worked. Emma took care of Keone at our home.

In March 1974, Chuck and I went back to Hotel Juraku on vacation and was asked by management to return for another summer engagement, but I had to decline this offer since we were being transferred back to the U.S. We were supposed to be in Guam for three years only. In the military, if you decided to stay longer than three years, everyone had to see a psychiatrist to make sure that they really wanted to stay in Guam and was not just "rock happy". When the Doctor asked me the reason I wanted to stay in Guam, I explained that I had a local Micronesian Revue and was making a lot of money. We lived on Guam from 1969-1974. It was a beautiful and wonderful experience!!!

I have had a lot of great opportunities during my life and feel very blessed!!! I have always treated everyone with respect and kindness, and it all came back to me!!! My group and I entertained at the Cliff Hotel until April 1974. We were transferred back to the U.S., Orlando, Florida, in May 1974.

★★★★★ *Never accept "no" from someone who is not in a position to say "yes".* ★★★★★

Chicken Kelaguen

4 Breasts of Chicken

Juice of 5 Lemons

1 c. Fresh Grated Coconut, not packaged

2 or 3 Red Hot Peppers

1 Small Sweet Onion, chopped fine

Salt, Pepper

- Boil chicken breasts for 10 minutes. Remove meat from bones and shred or put through coarse food chopper. Mix with rest of ingredients. (Hot peppers may be omitted).

Finadene

1 Medium Onion, sliced

3 to 6 Hot Peppers

1/2 c. soy sauce

1/2 c.Vinegar or Lemon Juice

- Mince or cut finely the hot peppers in a small bowl.
- Add the onions and the soy sauce.
- Stir in the vinegar or the lemon juice according to taste.

Enjoy these 2 authentic dishes from Guam!!!

7

Back To The USA: Orlando Micronesian Revue

We left Guam for Orlando, FL, in May 1974. We flew to Hawaii and visited my Mom and family for one week then flew to California and was met by my sister, Carolyn & her husband, Jay, and family. We stayed at Carolyn's home in Fremont, CA, for one week, and visited then Chuck drove to San Francisco to pick up our new 1974 Blue Ford Torino 9-passenger Station Wagon that we had purchased thru the Guam Navy Credit Union and we drove to Orlando, Fl, with a few days in DeKalb, Mississippi, to meet Chuck's Mom & family. That was quite an adventure to drive to Orlando and if we were not related, we would not have been friends when we got here being together in our car for such a long trip.

We stayed in temporary military housing until our home on McCoy Navy Housing was ready. We moved into Navy Housing shortly & got an unfurnished 4-bedroom home with 2 baths. There was a very nice Bowling Alley, Theatre, Post Office, Convenience Store, the Navy Exchange (like a department store), Commissary (grocery store), & Youth Center on the Base so that our children could go there & have all kinds of activities for them after school and on weekends. Hellen K., a beautiful and great positive leader, was the Youth Center Director, who everyone loved like a Mom. About four months later, I decided to start teaching Polynesian Dancing there and taught from ages 7 - 45. I taught two classes on Wednesday afternoon for an hour for the children and two hours for the teens and adults between 15 - 45. The teens and adults were very good, and I started training them to be in my newest Micronesian Revue. It took six months before our first performance.

We performed at the USO Shows for seven years from 1977-1983 twice a year and any Navy Hospital Functions so that the dancers could get some exposure and experience!!! The USO Shows were our favorite as we entertained over 2,000 recruits, 18 and over, each show 90 % men and 10%

women. They would scream and applaud with wolf calls and whistling as we set up our implements to dance before the show as the curtain on stage was about 5 inches above the stage floor and they could see our feet. We loved all that attention!!! We started to perform in the Enlisted Men's Family Club on the Base, the Club Mariner Enlisted Men's Club and the Officers Club on Naval Training Center in Orlando from 1975 and Naval Hospital Christmas Party in 1983.

In 1977, I wanted to build a float for a parade in Orlando. We all pitched in and one of the Mom's, Jo B., got us a flatbed trailer for the float and our Youth Center Director, Hellen K., got the place to decorate our float which was empty and under the Navy at that time and used by Eastern Airlines to fix their planes. Everyone, including the dancers, drummers, the Royal Court, parents, and anyone on the float, went to get greenery like palmetto palm leaves and flowers which were decorated on the float. It looked beautiful!!! Helen D., one of our dancers, worked for Orlando Federal Savings Company who sponsored us.

We also built another float for the Orlando Christmas Parade and Pine Hills Christmas Parade and the Boy Scouts Parade in 1977 and looked very pretty but we froze our okoles off during the Christmas Parades wearing our very colorful & skimpy Polynesian outfits!!! So that was on my bucket list of things to do and my group and I made that wish come true!!!

During the years 1976-1978, we performed for Central Florida Fair three times a week for two weeks in February and March. We were also featured in another big event for Orlando, "Fiesta-in-the Park" at Lake Eola in November from 1976-1978 and performed for the 4th of July Fireworks Celebration "Picnic in the Park" at Lake Eola for 1978.

Our other engagements were for the "Freedom Train Celebration" in 1976, Winter Park Mall's Cruise Show, 1976; Orlando Fashion Square's Festival of Nations, and Orlando Fashion Square's Christmas Show, 1977; Cerebral Palsy Telethon, 1975, 1976 & 1979; Firemen's Ball, 1978; Hyatt Hotel House Conventions, 1977 & 1978; Miracle City Mall, Titusville, Fl., 1979; Xanadu Night Club in Winter Park, 1979; Eastern Airlines Christmas Party, 1982; and Orlando International Airport's, «Up, Up, & Away" Airport Art Show, 1984. These were the shows that stood out and we had many more. Another fave fun gig was when we were hired to do two nights at the Happy Dolphin Inn in The Indigo Restaurant & Lounge at St. Pete Beach. I actually drove my Torino Station Wagon down

Janice, Theresa, Michelle, Monica, Shelly, Kathy
The Last Micronesian Revue

there in a caravan, with a small RV with all of our costumes and band instruments and another car driven by parents. That's when I was younger and didn't mind driving on long trips. Today I try to keep my driving in a 10-mile radius at the most. Too many crazy and impatient tourists that are very careless.

We performed on Friday & Saturday nights at 9 pm & 11 pm. The hotel gave us four rooms for our group of 12. We ate lunch and dinner in the hotel restaurant and that included Shrimp & Lobster/Steak Dinners. We were a big hit & they loved us!!! Getting paid to go to perform at a beach hotel is the best!!!

It took a lot of blood, sweat and tears to manage the Micronesian Revue starting with picking out the right team to train for the Revue, training the dancers who had never danced before including my children, designing our costumes, teaching the dancers how to sew their costumes, and practicing twice sometimes three times a week for our shows. I am a great admirer of families that perform together. I used to have my group watch videos of the Osmond Brothers so they could observe how the Brothers performed and moved together professionally!!! I was the Owner, General Manager, Instructor, Choreographer, and Mistress of Ceremony for the Revue. I also played the Keyboard, Ukulele, sang, was the Soloist Hula Dancer and Blindfold Samoan Knife Dancer and also played the toere for our tahitian oteas. I had to be able to do everything and be able to improvise the show in case a person got sick before the show, got in an accident or was late because of the traffic. Everyone had to be there one hour before the show so I could improvise if I had to. Sounds stressful??? You bet but I loved what I was doing, and it made my group and me have a very good feeling of exhilarations of each performance that was well done!!!

*****You have to eat, sleep and love your passion and dream for the future to make it happen!!! It will take a lot of work, blood, sweat and tears but it will definitely be worth it!!! *****

Hawaiian Beef Stew

Ingredients	Sauce
2 lbs. Beef Stew Meat	3 tsp. salt
1 Sweet Round Onion	4 tsp. sugar
2 Stalks Celery	4 T. cornstarch
1 lb. Baby Carrots (cut & peeled)	8 T. Soy Sauce
3 Large Potatoes or 9 Baby Dutch	(Aloha brand)
Yellow Potatoes	

- Add sauce to beef stew meat. Mix and let it marinate for 15 min. Brown in olive oil, drain oil.
- Add boiling water to cover the beef and cook for about 3 hours or almost tender.
- Add the rest of ingredients and cook for about 1 hour, or until vegetables are tender.

If you are in a rush, you can cook the beef in a pressure cooker & cook the vegetables (add more varieties if you prefer) in the microwave till tender. I usually thicken the stew with cornstarch and water. Do not freeze after adding cornstarch. It usually lasts for 2 days only for 2 people. Really ono!!! Serve over rice or mashed potatoes.

8

My Second Wish: Cruises

I had an interest in performing with our group on the Cruise Ships. I sent in resumes to several cruise ships and always watched "The Love Boat" on television with my children every week, and it became a wish I wanted to fulfill. One evening we were watching Love Boat and my husband got in from work and asked us what we were watching. I said Love Boat. I also told him that I'm going to get my group on a cruise and we weren't going to pay for it. He told me that would never happen.

The very next day, July 19, 1977, about 4:00 pm, I was cooking chili for dinner and the phone rang and my son, Keni, answered the phone. Keni said someone from the Cruise Lines wants to talk with you. I said, Yeh, right!!! The voice on the other end identified himself as a representative from Costa Cruise Line, Felipe C., and asked me if I was still interested in entertaining on the cruise ships. I replied, Is this a joke??? Felipe said, no and we would like to attend one of your shows so we can see if your show is what we need. Felipe and another representative flew to Orlando from

Miami the next day and watched our show that evening. He said they were looking for a group to entertain twice a week, 10 minutes each performance. We were going to entertain passengers from Caracas, Venezuela, who didn't speak or understand English. We would be part of a variety show which included an Indian Couple Knife Thrower, A Magician, A Singer/Comedian and our revue.

After our performance, we were hired and had to be in Puerto Rico in two weeks, August 4, to sail on August 5. We would be doing 7-day cruises to the Caribbean Islands from Saturday to Saturday and Puerto Rico was our home port. We were paid a salary plus lodging, meals, port charges and tips for the crew personnel which included our cabin cleaners, our dining room waiters and our Maitre D. When we weren't entertaining, we were passengers on the cruise. It was a great and wonderful gig!!! We actually volunteered to help the Cruise Director and staff on our nights off and enjoyed doing that. Whenever the Band played and no one would start dancing, the Band would come to our cabins and ask us to come and teach our line dancing to break the ice with the passengers.

Our group included my daughters, Mataiva and Michelle and three additional dancers: Denise, Shelly & Vicki and my sons, Keni, Samoan Knife Dancer, drummer and Keone, 8, who blew the conch shell and cleared our implements from the stage after our dance. Everyone, with the exception of Vicki, was under the age of 17. l had a meeting with the parents and had them sign a release form for me to take the dancers on the cruises. I set strict rules as a dress code which included no cut offs or jeans with holes and to always look presentable while we were in public. I also set a curfew on the ship that made everyone go to bed and leave the show room/ night club whenever I went to bed. No one was allowed to sit at the bar; they had to sit at the tables. They were allowed to roam free like going to the pool, sitting in the show room during the day, playing shuffle board on a special deck for the crew, etc., but everyone had to check in and eat our meals together so that I knew where they were. Michelle and Keone were always near or with me.

Our group had to be in Puerto Rico in two weeks. My group was excited and ready to do this. We rehearsed and packed and was ready!!! Costa flew us from Orlando (MCO) non-stop to Puerto Rico on Eastern Airlines. I had never heard of Eastern Airlines and the service and personnel were outstanding!!! Who would have known that I was going to work for them in the future. We had 25 pieces of luggage which included our costumes and props. This was a new experience for us, and we were very excited!!! We took 2 large vans from San Juan Airport to the pier to our first cruise ship, Costa Flavia. The Costa Line Ships were named after their daughters, Flavia and Carla C.

First Cruise Ship: *Costa Flavia*

August 5, 1977, Gross Tons 16,000

We all went out on the deck to watch us sail and learned that when the ship was scheduled to leave at 4:00 pm, the gangplank was pulled at 3:45 pm and the ship was away from the dock at 4:00 pm. Anyone that missed the sailing would have to fly to their first port of call to meet the ship at their expense!!! We had to be on the ship two hours before sailing. Your vacation starts as soon as you board. The breeze of the wind in our hair around us felt so good and was so exciting!!! An hour after we left port, everyone had to get their lifejackets from their rooms and assemble in a designated area for a briefing and fire drill. After that, we went back to our cabins and checked out the ship.

We had 3 cabins and ate in a special dining room for the entertainers, the band, the Cruise Director, staff and the officers. Our dining room was very large and we were assigned two waiters, Stefan and Roberto, at breakfast and dinner. We were served like the passengers were served in the main dining room. We ate breakfast and dinner in our dining room and lunch and tea were served on the deck with everyone else. We also ate the midnight buffet with the passengers in the informal dining room on the higher inside Lido Deck. Room service was available if you didn't want to eat dinner in the formal dining room; in fact, room service was available most of the day till 11:00 pm.

Our cabins were on the sea level and we could hear the water as we sailed. Our rooms smelled like diesel and had no windows. Keni, Michelle and Vicki were in one cabin; Denise and Shelly were in another cabin which Mataiva would share with them as soon as she met us on the 2nd cruise. Mataiva couldn't join us sooner as she was dancing with The Drums of Tahiti Luau Show at Sea World; Keone and I were in a cabin. The first night we sailed, the dancers and I took our

blankets and pillows and slept on the deck chairs on the pool deck where the fresh breeze could blow on our faces and keep us from getting seasick from smelling the diesel. Keni, Michelle and Keone slept in the cabin as they were too young to be out on the deck and I didn't want to lose them from sleep walking or just roaming around. At 6:30 am, we woke up early while the decks were being washed down and went back to our cabins. We did this for the first 3 nights and then got used to the motion of the ocean. The first morning we woke up at sea, everyone in our group was seasick except Shelly and Keone. Everyone had to go to the infirmary for a shot to help us with our seasickness. We had to be fine or we would have been sent home. In fact, that's how we got our opportunity to entertain on the ship because the group that we replaced got seasick and couldn't perform.

Our ports of call on the Flavia were San Juan, At Sea, Curacao, Trinidad, Martinique, St. Thomas, Caracas, Venezuela; and back to San Juan. We rehearsed after breakfast which was at 8:00 am. After that we had free time and just had to meet for lunch and dinner. The lunch buffet was between 11:30 pm-1:30 pm and served by the pool which included hot dogs, hamburgers, salads, chips, desserts, drinks, etc., or lunch in the main dining room was at 12:00 pm. We usually ate lunch by the pool as we were usually laying out and enjoying the band playing calypso music.

Keone was only 8 years old and he explored the ship and made friends with the cooks who taught him how to make his own rolls and bread; the ship photographers that he hung out with, and sometimes he would make friends with the Chief Engineer who showed him around the engine room. Keone told me that he saw the crew throwing old bread and rolls off the aft of the ship at sea and was invited to join them. At 4:00 pm-5:00 pm, it was tea and Patisserie time which had every imaginable dessert on the Lido Deck. The Maitre D. liked Keone and allowed him to get me about 3 different pastries that Keone thought I would like and say to me, "Look, Mom, what I got for you!!!" If I didn't like his choice, Keone would say, "Can I have it???"

Shocking News in Caracas, Venezuela: Overbooked Ship

On our way back to Puerto Rico, we were ending with some US citizens and picking up the first Venezuelan passengers. That's the first time I learned the meaning of "OVERBOOKED". OMG, after explaining the meaning of that word, we were told that we would be left in Caracas for one week and the ship would return for us. The staff left one of their cocktail waitress, Theresa, who interpreted for us as they only spoke Spanish there. We were put in an oceanfront hotel and all we did was rehearse a couple of days and the rest of the time we were tourists. We went into Caracas one day only as we were told it was not safe there. We took a bus into the city and, on our way home, were told when we wanted to get off the bus, just clap once. Well, when we saw our hotel, we weren't taking any chances of missing our stop, so our entire group clapped like an applause and got off the bus. At the hotel, I learned that Tia Marie was like Kahlua which I liked as it tastes like coffee. I used to drink that with whip cream. In a week, the Flavia returned to take us to Puerto Rico to get on our new ship, the Carla C. where we would be joined by my daughter, Mataiva, another dancer.

Second Cruise Ship: *Costa Carla C*

20,000 Gross Tons

The Carla C. was a larger ship than the Flavia and more modern. Our Ports of Call were San Juan, Curacao, Caracas, Venezuela; Trinidad, Martinique, St. Thomas, and back to San Juan. The room where we entertained, The OBSERVATION LOUNGE, was larger than the Flavia's Show Room and so were the dining rooms, the BOUTIQUE, and the CINE with movies at 2:00 pm, 8:15 pm and 10:30 pm. There were activities going on all day and you just chose the ones you wanted to attend. There was also a CASINO, BARBER SHOP, BEAUTY SHOP, MASSAGE & PEDICURE, GYMNASIUM, a BANK, the OBSERVATION LOUNGE where information of the tours on the islands and to purchase the tours, AGUA-SPORTS, the HOSPITAL, PHARMACY, PHOTO STUDIO, and A ROOM FOR CHILDREN ACTIVITIES. We performed in the OBSERVATION LOUNGE and the GRAND SALON was where they also had Bingo, COCKTAIL MUSIC and DANCING before dinner. One day, Keni told me to talk to Keone because he was running thru the halls with the Venezuelan kids yelling "Mafia, Mafia!!!" That wasn't too cool as we were on an Italian ship doing that!!! All the families on the Venezuelan cruises came from affluent families.

In August, we had two new ports added to our cruises: Miami and Port Canaveral where the passengers went to Disney World all day. In Miami, they had a tour to

SEAQUARIUM and shopping and at 7:00 pm, we sailed to PORT CANAVERAL so that everyone could go to DISNEY WORLD. Since Orlando was our home, we went home to visit our families and wash clothes and the kids visited their friends. We had to be back on the ship at 9:00 pm as we sailed back to Puerto Rico at 11:00 pm. Our Show was the next evening at 10:30 pm in the OBSERVATION LOUNGE with dancing after that. At 11:45 pm, the Fiesta Buffet Tropical Buffet was served in the Lido Room with the band, Criollo and the Cinco Aces. A Program was delivered to everyone's door every morning of all the activities for the day. It was all in Spanish and all we had to know was where the shops, the restaurants, the hospital and Pharmacy, the Pool and anything else that was important like where the meals were served and available and what time we performed. We usually rehearsed with the ship's band for our show about 10 am on the day of our performance. I sang & played the keyboard & performed as the Samoan Knife Dancer (Blindfolded). Keni, our Stage Manager, played the drums & also performed as the Samoan Knife Dancer. Keone, our Assistant Stage Manager, blew the Shell, set up & retrieved our instruments and implements. The ship's band, which consisted of drums, a bass guitar and an electric guitar, backed our Revue using my musical arrangements.

Our last cruise for the summer was September 9, 1977, where we sailed from Miami to Port Canaveral. Channel 9 camera crew and my husband, Chuck, cruised with us from Miami as they were doing a show for kids on Sundays called "Kids World" featuring Michelle, Keone and the rest of our group. They videoed our Revue and also the next morning of us eating breakfast before we docked at Port Canaveral. It was viewed on TV on a Sunday and I was given a copy of the video. That was a nice treat for all of us!!! We were sad to say bye to the entire crew and staff and it was time to go back home and the kids had to go to school. Michelle said that they missed about two weeks of school, but it was worth it!!! Can you believe what a dream job we had!!! This was the BEST JOB OF A LIFETIME!!! How many people get this opportunity??? I was very fortunate that I had my children who also entertained on the cruise with me.

Third Cruise Ship: *Italia*

March 21, 1978
Gross Tons 12,000

In the spring of 1978, we were asked to go on the cruise ship, the *ITALIA*, which was the smallest ship we had worked. A Canadian Company chartered the ship for two cruises for their employees. I thought that was extremely nice!!! We flew to Puerto Rico and embarked on the Italia on March 21 which had actually ended the first cruise on March 22. We entertained the passengers on March 21 since they were going home on March 22. We stayed in Puerto Rico until March 23 then sailed for St. Thomas at 1:00 am. The passengers were French/Canadian and spoke English, yea!!!

The following is a brief itinerary of our cruise. We entertained with a 45-minute Revue starting at 11:00 pm, 12:00 am was the Midnight Buffet, then sailed for St. Thomas at 1:00 am.

The *Italia* had a Hospital, Boutique, Beauty Salon, Photo Shop, Radio Station, A Cinema, A Disco, "LA CAVE DES PIRATES", and a large Showroom, "LE GRAD SALON" for the Entertainment Groups and our Micronesian Revue.

Ports of call for the *Italia* were: San Juan, St. Thomas, St. Maarten, Guadalupe, St. Lucia, Barbados, Grenada for their 10-Day Cruise. The Italia rocked and swayed a lot when it was windy one day and while we were rehearsing. Thank, God, it was calm when we entertained that evening. We spent the day at Curacao with the Band, Cruise Director and some of the staff. We sailed for Aruba, Miami and Port Canaveral,

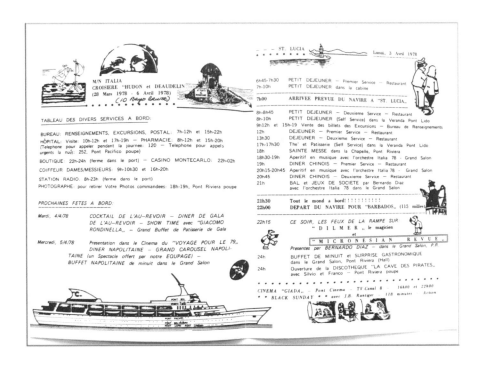

and drove back home to Orlando!!! We enjoyed our Spring Break and felt very blessed to do this again!!!

This picture is the program for the daily cruise.

⋆ *Don't fill out any surveys or enter any contests especially at conventions. You won't win and your phone number and email address are sold to solicitors and scammers. Nothing is free!!! Read the fine print!!!* ⋆

Kanoe's Macaroni Salad

INGREDIENTS

1 lb. Small elbow macaroni, cooked and drained★★

7 Hard boiled eggs, diced

2 cans Peas & Carrots (14.5 oz. per can), drained

2 cans Chuck Light Tuna (5 oz. per can), drained★★★

1/2 Sweet Round Onion, diced

2 1/2 cups Hellmann's Light Mayonnaise

- Mix the hard boiled eggs & round onion with the warm elbow macaroni
- Mix in peas & carrots and tuna
- Add mayonnaise and mix well, add salt & pepper to taste

★★ Boiled potatoes may be substituted

★★★ Sweet crab meat or 13 oz. can Chicken Breast, drained. Make it a day in advance & add more mayo the next day if the salad seems dry from the macaroni soaking up the mayo. This salad will last 7 days; however, if you are using for Pot Luck, one hour only!!!

9

My Third Wish: Airlines

Eastern Airlines
10/79-01/91

*M*y opportunity to fill my third wish was when my daughter, Michelle, babysat Keone's classmate, Russell, whose Mom, Jean R., worked at the airport. Jean was wearing an airline uniform and I asked her who she worked for. Jean worked at Eastern Airlines which was a coincidence as Eastern Airlines flew my Micronesian Revue & me to Puerto Rico when we were hired to perform on the Costa Line Cruise Ships. I asked Jean if Eastern was hiring & she said yes & would get me an application. The next day, Jean gave me the application and told me I could use her as a reference and she would take it in and give it to the secretary, Joyce A.

I gave Jean my application the following day and got a phone call within two days for a local interview with the Passenger Services Manager, Larry H., at the airport. I did well at my interview and was scheduled to go to Miami for three weeks of training and if I passed my exams, I would be hired at the end of my training. I was given a book with all the Eastern's city codes, both domestic and international, and would be tested on our first day of training. I purchased index cards and put the codes on one side and the cities on the other side to help me remember and be ready for my first exam.

My training was scheduled the following week in Miami. There were 20 girls in our class, and we stayed in 2-bedroom bungalows, two in each bedroom, with 2 baths, with a living room, dining room and kitchen. There were five bungalows. We ate our meals in the cafeteria which were healthy and delicious. We were paid $1.00 per day as a token and if we passed our exams, we would be hired as customer service representatives also referred as airport agents. Everyone in our class were from different occupations as travel agents, hairdressers, secretaries, waitresses, store clerks and surprisingly, none from the airlines. We all studied together and wanted to be sure we passed this course.

We were trained making reservations, selling special services like unaccompanied minors (UAM), selling upgrades, selling pre-paid tickets, etc., where a person would pay for the ticket at one destination for another person traveling from another destination. We also were trained in selling connection flights that were delayed or cancelled, booking hotel rooms when needed, collecting for overweight bags or extra bags and many other things that were needed. There was a lot of things to learn in 3 weeks.

The first day of training we were tested for over 100 EA city codes. Everyone passed and that was a good start for all of us. We had an hour for lunch then back to class. Our class started at 8:00 a.m. until 5:00 p.m. with a 15-minute break in the morning and one in the afternoon. After school, we went home and freshened up then went for dinner. After dinner, we went back to our bungalows for some serious studying!!! At the mid-point, 1 1/2 weeks, we had a mid-exam. After the exam, we went for lunch and if a person didn't pass the exam and didn't return to class, she was sent home. Only one person didn't return to class.

The following weeks, we had learned more and then our last week before we graduated, we went to fit for uniforms. That was very exciting as we were all so excited to work for Eastern. We were given our first set of uniforms which included different pieces, slacks, a skirt, four blouses, a dress, two blazers, a sweater and accessories so we could wear different styles. Our last day we had our final exam and then took a graduation group picture, picked up our uniforms then rushed to the airport to fly home. It was an exciting day, and I was very glad to fly home to see my family and sleep in my own bed. I spent all my days off making up my own Book with my notes from my class to help me at my new exciting career!!!

I started to work on Monday and was so proud and pumped!!! I started working on the Ticket Counter as a part-timer. It's different when I was in a classroom and scary when I had real people standing in front of me. The passengers were very nice, understanding and patient!!! Everyday got better and I became more confident and not as nervous. All the employees were very helpful, very knowledgeable and had a lot of seniority. All Part-Timers' seniority were based according to the amount of hours that we worked. I started with a 20-hours per week schedule and was able to pick up overtime and I loved every minute of it!!! Our benefits included medical benefits, vacation, sick leave, and my very favorite…travel benefits. This was the beginning of my 3rd wish!!!

I worked at different positions at the Ticket Counter and the Information Position. I also helped to relieve the agents in the Ionosphere Club, which was an Elite Eastern Airlines Lounge Club where the passengers with a membership would relax and get snacks and drinks before their flights. Our Club was located by the Ticket Counter and there were no long lines going to the gates, no TSA, and everything was at a slower pace without anyone having to go thru a security check. Today, the Airline Clubs are located in the gate area so that the passengers could relax before their flights without worrying about the long TSA lines. It is always stressful going thru the long TSA lines, originated after 9-11, as sometimes it takes 1-2 hours.

Eastern was the largest airline in Orlando in 1971 and was awarded Walt Disney World's Official Airline that had the Disney characters Mickey Mouse, Minnie Mouse, Pluto, Donald Duck and even Chip and Dale meet and greet certain arriving and departing flights. We had a great time entertaining the passengers especially the children. Eastern also had a people mover ride displaying Destinations at Disney World called, "If You Had Wings".

EA 003: Flight to the North Pole

During a Saturday in December, Eastern sponsored a "Flight to No Where" for some special children with terminal illnesses and children that were abused and their families that were selected by the Silver Liners, consisting of EA Flight

Attendants, that would actually board the aircraft with the children and their families which was a big deal and special as some of them had never been on a flight before. The Eastern flight crew flew them towards Tampa where they could observe Sea World, The Magic Kingdom and Kennedy Space Center from the air and then return to Orlando. Santa and the Disney characters gave the children gifts and candies when they returned to Orlando. A lot of people would volunteer for this including the employees on their days off. Some of the employee volunteers on the flight included Hal East, who videotaped the flight and event; our Trainer, Becky Smith and one of our Supervisors, Bill Lane. It was a wonderful annual event that everyone enjoyed and looked forward to!!!

Departure Gates

When I started working at the Gates, I remember meeting an upbeat and very friendly Customer Service Representative that wore a Red Coat, Danny D., and was very impressed by him!!! I asked Danny what were his duties which were assisting people and children with special services such as providing wheelchairs, escorting them to the flight, accompanying children who flew unaccompanied, etc. I loved this and I wanted to wear a red coat. I asked Danny how I could apply for that position and gradually applied for that position and wanted to be just like Danny. I worked at Eastern for a year then got laid off with being on the "On Call List" which meant that whenever Eastern needed extra help, I could be called in to work. We were called and could turn it down especially if we had another job; however, if we turned it down three times in a row, we were terminated. Eastern would give us enough time to plan for it like 2-4 weeks' notice to cover the heavy loads during the holidays or to cover the vacations.

Walt Disney Travel (WDT)

9/80-6/82

Walt Disney Travel was interviewing for a Travel Agent's position and I was asked to apply for that position. There were 17 Eastern applicants, and I was awarded that position. Working there was a different experience from the airlines. I worked at the desk greeting walk in customers that were interested in going on a short or weekend trip while here in Florida. People would walk in and tell me…I have 3 days and $2,000.00 dollars, where would you suggest that I could go??? It was usually Key West, Miami, and a lot of beach resorts, a cruise, a ranch, etc. I would suggest going somewhere with beaches which was drivable or fly to a ranch where a person could fly to a hotel with inclusive meals, some drinks, tours, etc. I did very well working there. As a travel agent, I had to research places to suggest then follow up on their plans till they left. It was like doing homework or researching places in addition to answering the phone and greeting more customers walking in off the street. I had good benefits working at WDT as my family and I got to go into the parks and had all the employee benefits. We wore costumes but were more relaxed with our makeup as long as we were neat in our appearance. Another perk was WDT dry cleaned all of our costumes to make sure we all looked good in appearance. The park employees' makeup were stricter than ours. The Head of Walt Disney Travel, ED, asked me to work for him full-time and not go back to Eastern. I politely declined and said thank you, but I loved to fly. At Eastern, we checked people in for their flights with their bags, they went to the gates and boarded their flights, and you would never see these people again as the majority of them were tourists with their families on vacation. Whenever there were delays, cancellations, etc., we worked with the passengers finding alternate cities. I definitely preferred working for Eastern. I helped one person at a time and I liked that better. After checking them in, I never saw them again at the Ticket Counter. All delays, cancellations, etc., were handled at the gates unless we knew ahead of time then we would handle them at the counter.

During the slow season, I was laid off for 2 months from Walt Disney Travel then was recalled back to work at WDT in charge of the SEAESCAPE CRUISES out of Port Canaveral for 6 months. I had two very good friends, Anita L. and Betty S., while I was working at WDT, and was invited to play co-ed volleyball for the Thursday night City of Orlando League by Anita, Captain of the Top Bananas. We needed more players so my daughter, Michelle, her boyfriend, Andy, and Robin, my BFF, all played for our team, The Top Bananas!!! We took the 1982 Fall League Champs & thank, God, I kept my trophy which helped me remember the date for my book. We played with 5 other teams and on Saturdays, we would all get together at my home and party!!! There were 3 boats and we would take turns on the boat on Lake Conway about 5 minutes from my home and the others would stay at my home and swim in my pool or relax in my hot tub with 5 people. We did this every weekend & loved to party!!!

Air Florida

11/83-8/84

I had to check for any job opportunities weekly while collecting unemployment compensation and one day I walked up to Air Florida and asked if they were hiring. The General Station Manager, Duane K., told me that he was looking for a temporary full-time agent to cover someone scheduled to go on maternity leave for six months. The six months became 25 months as someone else had to take a leave of absence. My schedule was four days a week, 10 hours a day with three days off. Wow, that was nice!!! Sounded good; however, after working for 4 days, I spent my first day off…sleeping and relaxing. I made a lot of friends there that were a younger group. Air Florida was a smaller airline with about 15 employees. It was a challenge to learn another computer for Air Florida after learning the computer systems for Eastern Airlines and Walt Disney Travel. I became very good friends with Robin P. who is still one of my BFFs today who works for another major airline. Robin and I both worked there until Air Florida went out of business.

Frontier Horizon Airlines

9/84-1/85

Frontier Horizon was starting service in Orlando and I was hired as a part-timer. We had to fly to Denver for three weeks training. Everyone had to be there on Saturday and I had to get special permission to fly there on Sunday since I was contracted a month before to put on my Micronesian Revue that Saturday evening at the Naval Training Officers Club.

When I arrived on Sunday afternoon, my roommate, Christine, who worked with me at Air Florida, greeted me and told me everyone was asking my age. I asked why and she said that seniority was based on our age. Christine told them she didn't know my age so on Monday morning, our first day of training, one of the students, Linda M., greeted me with "How old are you???" I asked her, "Why how old are you???" Linda told me her age, hoping she was older than me. I smiled and winked at her and said, "I win!!!" I was 3 years older than her. That meant when the shifts were posted for work, I got to bid first!!! Training was basically like the other airlines I worked for except the big challenge was to learn another computer system. We were offered 20 standby passes for $65.00 each which we could give/sell to our friends and family anywhere that Frontier Horizon flew in the US. I gave them to my relatives so that they could come and visit me in Orlando. Frontier Horizon was a small airline with less than 10 employees in Orlando.

Midway Express Airlines

10/84–06/86

I worked at Frontier Horizon for a month then my former employer and Manager of Air Florida, Duane K., called me at home and asked me if I would work for him also. Duane said that Air Florida was bought by Midway Express Airlines and all the employees that worked for him bid the morning shifts and he didn't have anyone on the night shift that had any experience. Air Florida and Frontier Horizon offices were across the hall from each other. I told Duane if he could get permission from Dan C., General Station Manager, of Frontier Horizon, and if he said it was okay, I would work for Midway Express.

Since I was the Senior Agent for bidding at Frontier Horizon, I bid the early morning shift from 6:00 am – 10:00 am. My shift was 6:00 pm – 10:00 pm at Midway Express since I was recalled before anyone new was hired which prevented interfering with my Frontier Horizon's shift.

Eventually, things slowed down at Frontier Horizon and I was asked if I would take the lay off since I worked for Midway Express and could allow the other employees to keep their airline job. I was given six weeks' severance pay. Well, God was watching over me because one week after I got laid off, Eastern Airlines called me back to work. So, at that point, I was collecting severance pay from Frontier Horizon, working part-time for Midway Express and full-time for Eastern Airlines!!! Wow, three paychecks from the airlines at one time!!!

Eastern Airlines
2/85-2/91

I went back to Eastern Airlines as a full-timer and started to work at the Gates and became a Red Coat Customer Service Agent. My other Red Coat team were Judy Thomas & Tammy I. We worked with Aida Diaz, Shift Manager, & Mike S., Supervisor, and were the trouble shooters. Whenever there was a delayed flight, cancelled flight, and irate passengers, we handled them. It was a great job which got stressful at times especially when the unhappy passengers yelled at us. So, this is the job that I wished for that Danny D. held and impressed me. That's how bad I wanted to wear a Red Coat which was my fave shade of bright red!!!

Working at the Eastern Gates were very exciting since we had a great group of employees down there. One of my fave Redcoats was Chuck C., who always had an upbeat personality, very intelligent & was very cool. Chuck always made sure we all ate well on our lunch break and would always cook for us!!! He was the best cook and I don't mean sandwiches. He prepared home cooked meals for us and made sure everyone at the Gates got to eat!!! My other Red Coats at the gate were Willie M., Tom H., and Paul M. who were all patient, professional and very knowledgeable like Chuck!!! Judy, Tammy and I basically worked the afternoon and evening shifts to cover the senior agents when they went home. The evening shifts were ugly at times because when a flight cancelled or was delayed, we stayed with those passengers until they gradually left on their flight or had to be rebooked for the next day and sent to hotels if it wasn't due to the weather.

Special Events and Moments to Remember "Give Kids the World"

Eastern employees volunteered to help build "Give Kids the World" Residence which was started and the land donated by HENRY LANDWIRTH in Kissimmee. This provided the families of terminally ill children a place to stay including other hotels who volunteered when they visited Disney World at no cost. Eastern employees, including myself, also built the children's playground with contributions from everyone. Budget Rent A Car would supply the Rental Cars for five days. Different foundations supplied tickets to Disney World, Sea World, Kennedy Space Center, and Baseball Spring Practice. These families were met and escorted upon arrival and departure.

Halloween

We were allowed to dress in costumes. I would always dress as a hula girl in a real ti-leaf skirt and would entertain the passengers at the Gate before their flights. I even got to meet a flight when they arrived and would go on the ramp, accompanied by an Eastern Ramp Man, who would flag the aircraft in as I danced in front of him dancing the flight in to the gate. The Captain would even tell the passengers to look out of their window to see a Hula Girl dancing as the plane taxied to the gate. I would run up to the jetway and as the door opened I would say…"Welcome to Hawaii….I mean Orlando!!!" The passengers were always happy and impressed with that!!! I loved doing that every year!!!

KLM, Royal Dutch Airline

1986-1990

Eastern had a contract with KLM working their flights twice a week. None of the senior agents wanted to work that because it involved part of the evening shift & they wanted to work only Eastern flights so that they could go home earlier. So needless to say, the most junior agents were assigned to KLM since we were the lowest on the seniority list. Working for KLM was nice and I loved their management team which consisted of the General Station Manager, Alan; Assistant Manager, Dan; and Joe G., Maintenance. They were strict and followed policy and our flights always left on time!!! The Station Manager & Assistant Manager were firm in dealing with the passengers whenever we had a problem. They didn't make any exceptions for anyone if it was about KLM's policy. The US Carriers try to accommodate the passengers and the passengers always try to intimidate or threaten the agents if they can't have their way. KLM Management was firm and followed policy especially if it was about safety and were always there for every flight!!! One incident I remember was when a passenger refused to check her bag at the gate because it had her medical X-rays in it and her bag was too large to carry on. This was before 9-11, so TSA wasn't operating yet. Alan spoke to her and told her the bag had to be checked. She refused to take out the X-rays and carry it on separately and Alan said she either check the bag or she was not flying. She cried and refused so he said shut the aircraft door. It was departure time and he was not going to argue with her. I admired how he handled that!!! She suffered the consequences and had to wait four days for the next flight and had to pay for a hotel till she departed!!!

My BFF, Linda Whetsel, worked at KLM with me. She and I became close friends as we were very Junior on the seniority list and helped each other at work. We made several trips to Hawaii with my children and she was the only haole (Caucasian) gal walking on Waikiki Beach with her Mickey Mouse Tee-Shirt, shorts and her tennis shoes. She was a great fan of Tom Selleck and Magnum, P.I. We also went to Las

Vegas and stayed at the Mirage and New York City to see the Xmas lights during December.

Eastern Went on Strike

March 14, 1989

International Association Machinists (IAM) Union had a dispute with Eastern for higher wages for the Ramp Service, Baggage Handlers and Aircraft Cleaners. Frank Borman, owner of Eastern, warned the (IAM) if they didn't reach an agreement before a certain deadline, he was going to sell Eastern Airlines. IAM and Eastern didn't reach an agreement so Frank Borman sold Eastern to Frank Lorenzo, Continental (CO) Holdings.

Eastern was still obligated to operate the KLM flights which was a blessing in disguise for our KLM agents. The KLM Station Manager, Alan, made sure that his KLM agents were working those flights and it allowed us junior agents to continue working with our benefits and pay!!! Some senior agents worked the flights by cleaning the planes, loading the baggage and anything else that was required. Eastern Management worked six days a week, 12 hour shifts with a skeleton crew.

Whenever I wasn't scheduled to work for KLM, I worked Security Duty with the guys which entailed driving on the runway to a remote area where our Eastern aircrafts were parked and just made sure no one was around the planes.

It was pitch black and we couldn't see anything without our van headlights or flashlights. It was very interesting & I hated the darn mosquitoes!!! We had to be heavily sprayed with insect repellant and even had some coiled mosquito repellant outside of our van.

After the Strike

06/89

Eastern returned into service under our new owner, Frank Lorenzo and Management. I started working in Baggage Services. That department was very special and unique in many ways. The majority of the people that we had contact with were not happy because their bag didn't arrive on their flight or was damaged. We had to trace everything by computer and phone calls which took longer.

Today the bags that are checked at the Counter or with Skycaps are scanned as it is loaded on the aircraft, and when it arrives at all connections before its final destination. If the bags don't arrive on the same flight as the passengers, it can be tracked and flown to its destination right away. I worked with the best night crew which included Paul M., Steve Y., and Gisele H. They were very knowledgeable, professional, polite and fun to work with and taught me everything about Baggage Services. They knew how to calm people and made a bad situation into a better situation and the people were somewhat satisfied most of the time!!!

I met a very nice Delta Baggage Agent, George Creech, who was very helpful in tracing our bags if they were in their Delta Tracing System whenever our bags would arrive on their Delta flights. He had a very nice announcer's voice on the PA system, and I told him that he should be a radio announcer. We became very good friends as he became my Delta connection whenever I needed help with their Baggage System. He had a very upbeat personality and was very knowledgeable in tracing bags. Everyone knew George and he was popular with our Baggage Service. He would call me and ask me if I was looking for an EA bag which came in on a Delta flight and would bring it over to us!!! I will always remember George for being a special friend and always being there for me whenever I needed his help. When I went for my first MRI, George offered to take me and sat in the room and just read his newspaper. Just knowing and hearing him turn the pages, made me feel more relaxed. George passed away August 2018 and is now an angel watching over us. George Creech was the Best!!!

In between flights when I wasn't busy, I also enjoyed taking pictures of the agents, skycaps and Management and made collages of MCO employees. I enjoyed doing this at our Christmas Parties, Halloween, and special occasions and made sure I had a roster of everyone so I wouldn't miss anyone.

Eastern was known as the best knowledgeable, polite and trained customer service agents that were kept up to date with our ticketing, gate, baggage and Operations skills by our trainer, Becky Smith. We had training classes whenever something new was introduced or updated. Becky impressed me so much that I wanted to become a Trainer in the future. Rich M. and John M., Supervisors, were also favorites of mine who left a great impression for their Airline and Customer Service Skills. They were the Bombs!!! Our Secretary, Joyce A., and Grace T., Admin Assistant, were always available and helpful!!!

From June 1989, Frank Lorenzo started to sell and transfer Eastern assets. Eastern finally closed its doors in January 1991. It was a sad day, but we all stayed on for two weeks so that we could rebook all future reservations on other airlines. We also had to be sure that all unfinished baggage claims were completed, and everyone was notified!!!

The night before my last flight departed, I bought a lottery ticket using my last flight number to Washington, DC., EA 858. I remember laying on the carpet at home as they announced those magic numbers. I jumped up and panicked about where I put my lottery ticket and then remembered I left it in my 280ZX. I quickly got the ticket and realized that I won $500.00. I decided to collect this at Publix since there were lots of people in the store.

The next day, Channel 2 was interviewing our passengers in line and asked me how I felt about us closing. I said I was very sad, but I had played my last flight number and won $500.00 and it made me happy. After we closed down and went to file for Unemployment Compensation, we were assigned a special room as our company had so many employees that were affected by this. They treated us special and made this transition a lot easier for all of us.

I will always have fond memories of my first airline, Eastern Airlines, who started my airline career. We were an excellent airline and are still remembered by many people. My daughter, Michelle, and her boyfriend, Andy, also worked at Eastern. Eastern made an impact on my son, Keone, because he started working at Delta and his wife, Cathy, works as a Flight Attendant for Delta. My nephew, Nappy N., and his wife, Dana, work as Flight Attendants for Alaska Airlines and my nephew, Sean S. is a Flight Attendant for Delta Airlines. You can see how much we all love working for the airlines. Eastern Airlines was my very first airline and just the beginning of my Third Wish!!! Eastern Retirees and Friends meet on the third Thursday of each month for breakfast and get caught up with the latest news about our airline and circle of friends.

P.S. A funny moment that happened at Eastern that is memorable!!! A passenger at the gate boarded on the wrong flight and the door was closed. The truck with the mobile stairs was driven away and it would have taken a while to get it back to the aircraft. The door was opened and one of our well-built Polynesian agents, Ovalo, also known as Pineapple, told the passenger to jump and he would catch him. It was a DC-9 which was our smallest Jet and the passenger hesitated but did jump and Ovalo caught him!!! Everyone remembers that!!! True story!!! That passenger had a lot of trust in Ovalo and Eastern.

Thank you, Eastern Airlines, Air Florida, Frontier Horizon, Midway Express, and KLM Royal Dutch Airlines for being part of my Third Wish and making this a wonderful experience for me!!! This was just the beginning of my airline journey.

Kanoe's Pig Cake

(2) Boxes Yellow Cake Mix

8 Eggs

Juice (2) cans mandarin oranges

1 cup oil

- Mix & add mandarin oranges
- Cut and line the pan bottom with a paper towel before pouring batter in
- Bake according to mix
- Sheet Cake -1 1/4 hours

2 doz. cup cakes 25-30 min.

TOPPING

1 pkg 5.1 oz Vanilla Jello Instant Pudding & Pie Filling

1 cup sifted powdered sugar

2 large cans Crushed Pineapple (drained)

- Fold in 16 oz. Cool Whip
- Refrigerate topping & frost cake before serving

Continental Airlines

03/1991 – 08/2008

I collected unemployment benefits for about a month after Eastern Airlines closed and was offered a part-time position with Continental Airlines. I asked the hiring Supervisor, J.R. Smith, if he was going to have another offer later and asked him if I could be considered to go to his next hiring session. I wanted to take a break as my sister, Carolyn, was coming to Orlando for a conference and I wanted to spend time with her. I asked J.R. how he got my phone number, and he said that Continental asked Eastern for a list of hirable employees. I was curious because I didn't apply for a position at Continental. Two weeks later, J.R. called me on Sunday evening at 8:30 pm and asked me if I would be interested in the position and if I was able to fly to Newark on Tuesday morning. I flew up to Newark and had to wait for my test results which took about two weeks. My son, Keone, who worked for Delta, asked me to go to Hawaii with him and this would have been a great break before going back to work. We flew over there for a week and got my test results when I returned.

I had to fly to Houston for two weeks' training with other Eastern Airlines employees. We had a special refresher class since we were experienced airline employees. The day I flew out, Matt Conrad, Admin Supervisor, told me by the time I returned from training, I would be a full-time agent, Wow, that was nice to hear!!!

When I returned home, I spent the weekends making up my own Airline Guide of all my notes from my training books and class. It basically covered checking passengers in for flights, rebooking reservations, selling tickets, special services, and selling pre-paid tickets also known as P.T.A. tickets. This became Kanoe's Red Book which everyone used. It was made of bright fluorescent index cards with all the formats and shortcuts for tickets, upgrades, additional charges for bags, telephone information, etc.

Soon after I got hired in March 1991, CO had a Woodstock theme party with Tie dyed shirts, outfits, etc., and I immediately knew this was a fun party group. It was a good way to break the ice for the 17 Eastern Airlines former employees who joined CO. We enjoyed this party and got acquainted with everyone.

I worked on the Ticket Counter for two months until we had to bid for a new work schedule or shift. Every 3 - 6 months, we had to bid according to Seniority for a new schedule since it was going to be summer and our flights would increase. After everyone bid, the last positions available were in Baggage Services which handles Delayed Baggage, Damaged Baggage and Lost and Found for CO. Our shifts were for the evening which began at 3:00 pm- 11:30 pm, 8 hours with a half hour for dinner. We also had two 15-minute breaks which we took in between our flights. We had to go to Baggage Services Training, and I started to make another White Book for Baggage. Yvette and I worked 5 days a week with part of the weekend off; Mark worked 4 nights with 3 days off during the week. Three other senior agents working the day shift were Catherine, Ray P. and our Red Coat, Viviana. We were very busy if any of the bags were left off the flight and would be arriving on the next flight. We had to fill out the Delayed Baggage Claim for each of the passengers who checked their bags and had it delivered to their hotels or homes whenever their bags arrived. Whenever the bags were left off the flight, we would get a message from that station to give us a heads up so we could page the people who were affected and start to fill out their baggage claim and not stand by the bag belt waiting for it. Sometimes we were lucky to get help from the ticket counter and gate agents who were clocking out, when management would make everyone stay for mandatory overtime.

Having Tuesdays off wasn't a bad deal for some of us. We would go to Disney's Pleasure Island which had night clubs with different themes to dance the night away. Tuesdays were Hospitality Night. Normally, it would cost $20.00 to get into Pleasure Island but on Tuesdays, it costs us $6.00. This included anyone working for the airlines, hotels, theme parks, restaurants, etc. We had our own CO group which included Nilo, Miguel, Nora, Judy C., Maggy, Patsy, Shauna, Tom, Karen B., Brett, Lisa, Thalia, Nilsa, Sharie, Chris, Angel, Angie, Cathy, Keone, John and me. Our fave club was 8-TRAX, 70's music. We would all meet there then go to the other clubs.... MANNEQUINS (Popular Electronic, Techno Type Music with a round moving dance floor), MOTION (Top 40's), JAZZ CLUB, NEON ARMADILLO, (Country & Western Club, Andrea from CO was always there) & THE COMEDY CLUB...just to name a few clubs. There were shows on the outside stages, parades, and dancing in the streets!!! It was a very happy place for a night of entertainment!!! An AMC Theater with 20 Large Screens, several shops & restaurants including "The House of Blues" and "Planet Hollywood" were outside of the gated Pleasure Island Clubs. We went there for years until they closed the clubs and made it into a restaurant row & shops!!! We had lots of fun and were a happy group!!! Did I mention that CO had a younger group that loved to party & enjoyed the night life??? Pleasure Island became Disney Springs.

During the summer of 1991, CO hired high school students called the Go-Getters to work with our special services program which included meeting and greeting the passengers in wheelchairs, escorting Unaccompanied Minors, assisting anyone needing extra help to go to and from the gates, upon arrivals to Baggage Services, and to their transportation. My fave Go-Getter was Michael M., who was always upbeat, helpful with a positive attitude!!! The Go-Getters were a great addition to CO & helped a lot during the summer.

We used to have long breaks between flights, and I would bring in my Sony Portable 8 mm VCR with cassette movies to keep us entertained. The Go-Getters loved to hang out with me in Baggage Services to watch the latest movies. They would even call me at home and ask me to bring in certain movies. We would sit in the Supervisor's office and pop popcorn and have sodas and all enjoy the movies. Between the flights, everyone would know that the Go-Getters were with me and knew how to locate them whenever they needed them. When the flights came in, we would all be ready to work and stop the movies till our next break.

We worked in Baggage Services for about 5 months and the Senior agents saw how much we enjoyed it there and decided to bid there so we ended up at the Ticket Counter. While I was at the Ticket Counter, I expanded my Red Book with all my Ticketing formats and information which helped me to become an ace ticket agent. My Red Book became very popular with everyone that they always used it for ticketing or any information which was easier than learning it from the computer in front of the customer. Even my Supervisors used it. I asked one of my fave Supes, Robert H., how he became a good ticketer and he told me it was from my book, he always used it. I wrote it in simple steps that anyone could follow it. It took me more than a month on my days off to make this book to make my job simpler and everyone loved using it too. The agents would ask me where was my book??? I asked them why they needed it, they would tell me and I would turn to the page they needed and tell them to follow all the steps and if they had a question, just ask me. They never had to ask me since I made it so simple and easy to issue anything that was needed. I would even have sample forms in it. I must admit, it was awesome!!! Later I even updated my Red Book to Kanoe's Green Book, Revised 2nd Edition, Best Seller.

Today things are much simpler. The computer is point and click and issuing tickets or reissuing tickets are a lot faster. So, no one needs a book like mine anymore.

Diane S., our Redcoat, and we were working at the ticket counter one evening & talking about having a Halloween Party. I offered to host the party at my home & that was the beginning of our wonderful CO Parties.

Everyone dressed in costumes and some were made up so well that I didn't even recognize them!!! My home was packed with CO friends & mechanics, my personal friends and families!!! My parties were so good that my children's college friends and parents would be there too!!! My home was known as the "Best Party House!!!" I had 11 speakers in my family room including two sub-woofers and sound surround system. I had laser lights, running lines, and a helicopter 8 round different lights that spun around to the music. It looked like a night club in my family room!!! I had the entertainment place where you could sing "Karaoke" in the Family Room that even scored the singer after each song which was fun & became a friendly competition to try to beat each other's score!!! Dancing to the 70's music and Latin music were on the Lanai, with our bartender, Nilo Escorcia, mixing mojitos and being our own DJ with the music cranked up!!! I even had disco lights pulsing to the music!!! Curfew time on weekends was 2:00 am and I made sure everyone was in the family room by 1:30 am to chill out before 2:00 am when the party was over!!!

All of my parties were Pot Luck & BYOB as I didn't drink or supply alcohol!!! I always made my famous "Hawaiian Kalua Pig" which would melt in your mouth, Hamburger Dip with Chips and home baked Blueberry Cream Cheese Cake or Pig Cake. Everyone brought different delicacies. About 10:00 pm, my daughter, Michelle and I, put on a mini Polynesian Show which was always a big hit!!! We also did "Last Dance" by Donna Summer using the black lights and poi balls. Coming to my parties was like going to a night club!!! It started at 6:00 pm and lasted till 2:00 am. Everyone stayed until 2:00 am.

Other airline employees included Delta Airlines, American Airlines, Midway Airlines, Orlando Police from the airport, and friends that worked at the Information Desk at the Airport. The Party Invitation was spread by word of mouth and we always had a packed house!!!

Lots of Opportunities for
Different Airline Positions:
Automated Streamlined Airport Processing
(A.S.A.P.) Facilitator

In August 1994, CO was looking for 21 Agents to become Facilitators/Instructors for their new Automated Streamlined Airport Processing (A.S.A.P.). These Instructors would be sent all over our CO system in the Continental USA. CO was also looking for Agents to teach, KASET, a new way of Specialized Customer Service. I decided to apply for both of these positions. Becoming an ASAP Instructor was my first choice. My interviews were scheduled for the same day, Friday, at 8:30 am. for ASAP and 11:30 am for KASET, a Customer Service Trainer at another location in Houston (IAH). I had to prepare for my ASAP interview by presenting a scenario of my choice.

I decided to pick a scenario that was difficult and not simple. I had an unaccompanied minor, 7-year-old female, Chelsea Souza, flying on a connecting flight from San Francisco (SFO) connecting at Houston (IAH) with a final destination at Orlando (MCO). Chelsea was flying on a pre-paid ticket, (ticket paid for by her Aunt in MCO), ordering a special child's meal and had an extra overweight bag. Unaccompanied Minors had to pay a fee so that CO would board and escort them to and from the aircraft, on the connecting flights, and arrival at their final destination. A prepaid ticket is when a person pays for a ticket from one destination like MCO to have another person fly from another origin like SFO. A pre-paid ticket took between 45 minutes to an hour to put all the information in the computer and collect the fee for the ticket. Today we use electronic tickets also known as E-Tickets which are a lot easier and faster to issue. All the information is taken from the parent regarding who is sending the child and also who is picking up the child at the destination. The parent or guardian takes the child to the gate and cannot leave the airport until the flight is in the air.

My interviewer was very impressed with me and when I asked her when would I get the results of my interview, she told me that I got the position. I wanted clarification on this and said I have another interview for the KASET Customer Service Trainer Position at 11:30 am. Are you telling me not to go to that interview??? Are you going to call them and tell them??? She said yes and they would also notify Orlando that I was selected as an ASAP Trainer. I was excited and flew back to Orlando.

I had just bid for my new shift and everyone from my position on the bid had to re-bid as someone would have wanted my line. I was so pumped up and excited to be selected as one of the 21 ASAP Instructors and felt very special!!! We all went to IAH for two weeks of training then we were sent to different cities in the U.S. to train the agents.

I always thought that traveling on business like our business passengers were very lucky to do this. I learned otherwise as they told me it was not fun!!! Here's my scoop of my experience on business traveling. It is a lot of work!!! Being an instructor meant preparing for the class before and after the class on our own time, eating meals by yourself as we were all sent to different cities to work, having hardly any time to fly home and fly back. I worked from Monday thru Friday noon. I got on a flight home on Friday afternoon. I was home about 3:00 pm, all day Saturday, and had to fly back on Sunday afternoon and had to prepare my class on Sunday afternoon in my classroom. I did this until December 1994 and had to fly home because I needed a root canal. Since it was closer to Christmas, I decided to spend Christmas at home. I was asked to go back to be a Trainer after New Years' and decided to go back to Orlando (MCO) Airport, my home station, and return to being an agent.

I was assigned a day shift with weekends off, the same as being an instructor, until the next bid and worked at the Ticket Counter. My experience about traveling on business was that I thought it would be nice to travel for work but have changed my mind. I enjoyed being at home and working at the airport. I loved going to work, going home to relax, watch TV, sleep in my own bed and have the freedom to get in my car and go anywhere. I definitely appreciated working locally and staying grounded near home. What's that saying… be careful what you wish for???

Continental Associate Trainer (CAT)

1/1998 - 12/2004

January 15, 1998, I applied for the Associate Trainer Position. My duties included willing to work a flexible schedule and providing training relief throughout the airport including the Ticket Counter, Baggage Services and Gate Departures. I scheduled the employees and Supervisors for training in Orlando and different cities for CO, America West, Gulfstream and vendors (private companies that worked under CO). I also booked their travel arrangements, hotel accommodations and their classes. I kept accurate records of everyone's training for our station (MCO) as we were audited by CO's system auditors and the Federal Aviation Administration (FAA) auditors to be sure we were current in FAA Security Directives. Audits were not scheduled. The auditors would always show up unannounced. I remember a weekend when I was off and at Disney. My Supe, Rick T., called me and told me that the auditors were there. Rick asked me where my training files were located, and I told him exactly where to find what files the Auditors were looking for and happy to report that we passed our audit!!! It pays off to be a detailed person and keep files up to date!!!

Customer Service
Representative (CSR)

A Customer Service Representative, also known as the RED COAT, handled over 95% of the problems with the customers. If the Red Coat was unable to satisfy the customer, the Supervisor would speak with our customer.

The main duties were to be in charge of the Ticket Counter and assist the agents with ticketing problems, baggage check in problems and anything that required special attention. We were the Supervisor's assistant. I was also an acting Supervisor, Airport Services, (SAS) whenever a Supervisor was on vacation or unavailable. The Departure Gates had several Red Coats and Baggage Service also had a Red Coat on duty.

CO also assigned a CSR/Red Coat to Virgin Atlantic as we did a code-share flight to London with them. CO had a group of seats blocked to sell in our computer system. On days of a Virgin Atlantic flight departure, our CSR would be present at their Ticket Counter to answer any questions about the flights that were purchased under CO. The CSR was also present at the Gate before departure.

CO also used to own 40% of COPA Airlines which flew to Panama, Central America, and our CO agents checked the passengers in at the Counter, then went to the Departure Gate and also handled any Lost Baggage. As a CSR, I also did

Security at the Gate and manually scanned each passenger as they boarded their flight.

At CO, some of the nicer things that I did was to escort celebrities like Michael Bolton, Patrick Ewing, George Forman, and Wesley Snipes to the Gates to pre-board their flight and introduce them to the flight crew and make sure they were comfortable before the General Boarding.

Complaint Resolution Official (CRO)

CSO is responsible for resolving any disability-related issues that have escalated beyond an initial interaction with airline personnel.

Ground Security Coordinator (GSC)

A CSR or Red Coat was responsible for the safety of the aircraft before departure. If there was a problem at the TSA (Transportation Security Administration) Point, we would go over to solve the problem with our customer. We would try to solve any problems before they left the Ticket Counter. There were also GSCs at the Gates to do this. The GSCs could prevent a passenger from flying if we felt it was a safety issue.

Uniform Coordinator

(1998-2008)

A Supervisor usually did this, but I was asked to assume this position at our station. I loved doing extra projects and this was very nice. I ordered uniforms, took measurements for both men and women, exchanged and returned uniforms and called the vendor (company that provided the uniforms) if there were any problems or questions and also called CO Houston Office regarding uniform standards and questions. MCO was chosen as a test city. We got to wear the new uniforms for a month, and I selected the testers in different sizes and worked closely with them about any problems or suggestions.

A cute story was when one of our male employees, Ric L., came into my office and asked me to measure his inseam for his trousers. I'm sure he just wanted to see my reaction to his request. Without showing a blushing re-action, I told him to lay on my desk on his side, lift up his leg and handed him one end of the tape measure and told him to put the end of the tape next to his body that he loved the best. He blushed and walked out of my office!!! When will these men learn not to mess with an older woman!!! I also appeared as a model displaying the uniforms for the Field Services Division: Ticket Counter, Gates and Baggage Service in our Uniform Catalog.

Fun Memories as an Associate Trainer

I had my own private office next to my Supe, Rick T., and decorated it in a fun, leisure and business atmosphere. My office tiered trays read "Now" on top, "Later" in the middle and "Sooner or Later" on the bottom. If Rick or anyone else needed something done now, I would just take care of it right away. I had my name on everything like my stapler, room fan, my books that I created for tips to work at the Ticket Counter, my paper clip holder, and anything that I could write my name on so it wouldn't leave my desk or if I saw it in the break room, I knew it was mine!!! The stapler was my favorite. I ordered office supplies and didn't like the new stapler because the older one had a pretty chrome base that I used as a mirror to re-apply my lipstick. One day, Rick, told me that he was working on reports with a deadline and did not want anyone to interrupt him unless it was an emergency, and he didn't want to shut the door to his office. You had to pass thru my office to get to him.

I decided to go to the Orlando Police Dept. in the airport and asked them to please give me that wide yellow and black tape that read "Crime Scene…Do Not Enter" and taped it across his doorway so no one could enter. He had to bend low to get past the tape to enter his office. Everyone who entered the hall behind the counter could see this to get to the Director's Office and our break room. It was funny!!! I didn't think of taking a pic of that!!! That would have been a Kodak Moment!!! It worked because no one needed him that badly!!!

The agents would ask me what was new that was happening in Rick's office and I told them, nothing!!! Agents would go to see him for Human Resources questions, etc. I knew how people liked to gossip and if I mentioned anything, they would all say "Kanoe said". I wasn't going to have anything labeled on me. Whenever I was asked anything that was "None of their Business", I said "Nothing; however, if I heard anyone was sleeping with another person, my ears would perk up!!!²

I loved working for CO and retired in September 2008!!! The employees at Orlando International Airport are awesome and very caring and did an excellent job!!! I give a lot of credit to our CEO Gordon Bethune who took our airline from "Worse to First". Gordon cared about us and we worked very hard to make our airline one of the best!!! We will always remember him and keep him in our wonderful memories at Continental Airlines!!! Gordon is the Best!!!

The following is my personal opinion that I would like to share:

Believe and trust your employees to do a good job, be very professional, be patient, make good decisions and help your customers be satisfied with your services, etc. Treat your employees like they are part of your family!!! Whenever your employees make your customers happy, the company makes money and gets a good reputation!!! When I say trust your employees, don't believe a total stranger that complains about your employee and take the angry or disgruntled customer's word without believing your employee's side of the situation. I have seen the morale of many outstanding employees go down because of management's decisions. If the employee has had a history of similar problems, go thru the steps of discipline. You are management, act like a fair management and protect your employees. Be fair!!! Stop picking on the good employees and showing favoritism to those who are making bad choices. Everyone knows who they are and that lowers the morale of the good employees!!! Most of the employees are proud to be a part of our company and do a good job because they love working for our company. Reward and promote those that deserve it!!!

Kanoe's Kalua Pig

6 lbs. Pork Butt

4 fl oz. Hickory Liquid Smoke (use about 1/2-3/4 bottle)

Hawaiian Salt or Coarse Sea Salt or Rock Salt

- Preheat oven 450 degrees.
- Make holes in Pork with a large fork & rub Liquid Smoke and Hawaiian Salt to season.
- Wrap Pork in green tea leaves & seal tightly w/ foil
- Place Pork in roasting pan (fat side up) and bake for 1 hour at 450 degrees.
- Lower oven to 400 degrees and bake another hour
- Lower oven to 300 and bake another hour
- Lower oven to 250 and let bake for 3 hours. After baking, shred Pork & sprinkle with 1 1/2 T. of Hawaiian salt and liquid from Pork.

Makes 12 servings. Without using it as a main course, it will serve more. The Pork can be frozen up to 6 months. The next day, fry with shredded head cabbage, and serve with rice. This is especially for Brigid who always asked for my recipe.

Kalua Pig in Crock-Pot

6 lbs. Pork Butt

Rub with Hawaiian Salt or Coarse Sea Salt or Rock Salt

4 fl oz. Hickory Liquid Smoke (use about 1/2 to -3/4 bottle)

- Pat Pork Butt dry
- Poke holes in Pork Butt & rub Hawaiian Salt & Liquid Smoke all over it
- Put just a little water in the bottom of crockpot.
- Layer the bottom & sides with clean washed ti leaves
- Add Pork Butt and put on low about 8 hours
- Cook till the Pork falls apart then shred & serve

Enjoy this recipe, Brigid!!!

Mahalo to my beautiful daughter-in-law, Melissa Souza, for sharing!!!

Riema's Ono Spaghetti Sauce

2 lbs. Hamburger

4 bottles Bertolli Vodka Sauce (24 oz. ea. Bottle)

1 sweet round onion diced

- Fry hamburger in 2 Tbsp. Olive Oil till brown & crumbly
- Add sweet onion, diced, fry till hamburger & onion are well done
- Add (4) bottles of Vodka Sauce
- Bring to boil then simmer on low for 3 hours stirring occasionally to prevent burning
- Serve over spaghetti

BON APETIT!!!

My family's fave Spaghetti Sauce which taste like I made this from scratch!!!

Always a request when they come to visit me!!!

Thank you, Riema, for sharing!!!

10

Retirement

I retired from Continental Airlines (CO) in 2008. I really didn't intend to work this long but I learned that if I didn't retire soon, I would lose $5,000.00 a month because of the tax rules and how I would be taxed. Retirement also feels like graduation from High School. I didn't have to get up early and go to school. My future days were free to do whatever I wanted to do.

My first thought was now I get to do a lot of things at home like getting rid of a lot of things and clothes that I had accumulated over the years. Sounds familiar??? Sounds good but so far I haven't really done anything. I finally figured out why I don't want to get rid of a lot of things & clothes. It's all about my memories of my past. I'm sure everyone has thought about this too. I'm sure I'll fit into my fave clothes that I wore in the '70's and the fashions will come back sooner or later. I keep telling myself that I have gotten into some of my clothes. Sounds familiar??? I have given some nice clothes away but not enough to see the results in my closet. Would you believe I have a room full of costumes from my Revue in the 70's that my grand-daughters fit in and use to dance whenever we perform???

Some of my Polynesian friends told me that Auntie Kau'i taught lessons and I should join them at the Polynesian Resort. It was hard to do while I was working because of my airline schedule change every six months. I decided it was time to go back to dancing now that I could commit and be there. Classes were twice a week and I really enjoyed learning new dances and making new Polynesian friends. There was something that I felt very uneasy about driving to Disney by myself. My BFF, Sandy B., would go with me to give me the confidence of driving there. I was not used to driving more than a 10-mile radius from my home. I lived 6 miles from the airport when I worked for CO so driving 22 miles each way to Disney was a little intimidating for me.

When I first started driving to Disney, I armed my car with a can of bee spray that could spray 25 feet away, a bull horn, a large flash light, pepper spray and a Taser!!! The Taser scared me when I tested it!!! A year later, I decided to buy a new 2010 Honda Accord to make me feel more comfortable!!! I was more afraid of getting stalled between Disney and before getting to I-4. Oh, hell, I didn't feel relaxed until I got off on Orange Blossom Trail (O.B.T.) My son, Keone, said it was more dangerous on OBT but I felt that there were stores, gas stations, and restaurants and the streets were lit up so I could wait for help in a lit area.

I finally met Auntie Kau'i, a beautiful Polynesian woman, who used to run the luau at Disney and worked as a Greeter at the Polynesian Resort with Kuulei and Lipoa. I became friends with her and a lot of her students and felt very welcomed and happy to be there.

Every third Saturday, the Polynesian Resort had a large hoolaulea (show) at 11:00 am – 12:30 pm featuring Auntie Kau'i's group and other halaus (students of other groups). Some of the groups featured were Kawehi's Halau, Aunty Mac's Halau from the Villages, Jet, Keawe and Cheryl's Halaus from Jacksonville, Debi's Halau from Apopka, Mililani's Halau from Cocoa Beach, Hilary's Halau from Melbourne, Space Coast Hula Ohana from Melbourne, and Aunty Otila from Tampa. There were 4-5 halaus featured each month. Tahiti Tamure, Orlando's Finest Tahitian Revue, would perform on special occasions.

Every July there is a Hoike (Hula, Tahitian and Samoan Knife) Competition at the Wyndham Hotel in Orlando where all the halaus would be invited. These groups were from Ft. Lauderdale, Melbourne, Cocoa Beach, Georgia, California, Japan, Virginia, Maryland and any group that would like to compete. This is an annual event originated by Uncle Hank Ohumukini and his family. I danced for these events until December 2011 when I was given an opportunity to go back to work for United Airlines (UA) in San Francisco. More details about Auntie Kau'i and the Hoike in "Special Friends" Chapter!!!

San Francisco (SFO)

01/2012 – 08/2012

Continental Airlines (CO) and United Airlines (UA) merged in 2012 and a group of retirees and active employees were selected to go to various cities mainly Chicago (ORD), Washington (IAD) and San Francisco (SFO). We were called The Success Team also referred to as the Passenger Service System (PSS) Team that were trained for this special assignment in ORD after 2 weeks training. We were there to assist and support the UA and CO Customer Service Agents in ORD, IAD, and SFO.

Most of the people were working in IAD and ORD. My BFF, Patricia, and I were assigned to SFO which felt very special since I asked to be assigned there. Our job was to stand behind the UA/CO agents and assist them whenever they had a question. We were not allowed to get on the computers, just to assist the agents.

It was difficult at first like blending two families (children and step-children). There was a lot of resentment between UA against CO. As time passed, we all got to become friends and it was easier to work together. The bottom line is we are one company and we all had to work together to make UA become successful!!! Patricia and I worked four nights a week with 3 days off. Our shift was 4:30 pm with two breaks and 1/2 hour for our dinner break. We were off at 2:00 am. We were both assigned to the Customer Service Center (CSC) which handled any problems like delays, cancellations, re-booking flights, arranging hotel accommodations and assisting passengers with anything else. We had a special hotel van pick us up after work as the hotel shuttle stopped running at 1:00 am.

We stayed in a hotel, Larkspur Landings, which was about 10 minutes from the airport. Our accommodations included a private room with a bath, kitchen, dining nook and also a desk/computer area. Our hotel provided us with a variety of breakfast goodies as little boxes of dry cereal, cartons of milk, OJ, string cheese sticks, fruits, tea, coffee, muffins, bagels, and different yogurts which we could eat in the dining area or take back to our room. Breakfast was served from 6:00 am till 9:00 am. I would get up by 8:00 am, go down to the lobby to get any breakfast goodies and take it back to my room so I could eat it later as I didn't have to go to work until 3:00 pm for a 4:30 pm shift. I would always go to work early and stop at Burger King to get me a Whopper Jr, French fries and a drink before work. We had to be in the conference room for our afternoon briefing before we started our shift.

On our days off, we were allowed to fly home which was nice but difficult even though we had positive space or confirmed reservations. It took one day to fly home, one day at home and one day to fly back to SFO. For me, it was more convenient to fly home once a month and just have my family pick up my mail, check on my home and water my plants. My neighbors, my son, Keone and our Belle Isle Police also helped to check on my home. My neighbors told me sometimes the Police were checking my home 3 times a day. I would bring them See's Candies or Hawaiian Chocolate Covered Macadamia Nuts in appreciation for doing this.

On our days off, Patricia and I spent one of our days going to SFO on Bay Area Rapid Transit (BART) which is a train going from the airport to SFO city and transfer to a trolley to go to Fishermen's Wharf to walk around and eat at the Seafood Restaurants and shop. As Seniors, we could purchase a ticket on the BART valued at $24.00 for $9.00. It was like a train and we would swipe our BART ticket and it would deduct our fare from it and when we used most of it, we would just buy another ticket. That was a great deal for us!!! We could go to SFO and just explore the city. The trolley's Senior Fare was 75 cents one way and if you returned within 3 hours, it was free to return using your transfer ticket to the Westfield Mall. The large anchor stores are Nordstrom which had two large Mitsubishi Circular Escalators that connected to the rest of the Mall, Macy's and Bloomingdales. Other stores near the Mall were Forever 21, Old Navy, and the Ferrari Store and many more popular stores and restaurants. Chinatown was also a fave place to shop.

I requested to be assigned to SFO because my sister, Carolyn, and my brother, Keoki, and their families and my cousins, Kammy and Ricky, lived there and I could spend time with them. My cuz, Kammy, would take Patricia and me grocery shopping and to Trader Joes once a week, then we would go out to lunch. Kammy also took us to Half Moon Bay for lunch at Sam's Chowder House, a famous restaurant located on the side of a cliff, and to the marina where fresh sea food was sold at the markets from the fishing boats. Kammy and her hubby, Russell, also took me to see my sister, Carolyn and her family while I was there. Sis Carolyn, my brother, Keoki, nephew, Derrick, and nieces, Lori and Julie came to SFO to visit me at my hotel and we went out to dinner.

When we started working there, our first good friend was Stephanie G., who was very friendly, helpful, and made us feel welcome to be there. She was the cutest, friendliest, petite person with the prettiest blonde curly locks. Stephanie offered to show us around SFO on our days off. She picked us up at our hotel in her Bright Chartreuse VW and drove us to downtown Fishermen's Wharf area which was very interesting. She was raised in SFO and knew all the interesting spots. She took us to The Ferry Building which had a spot to eat that made the best rotisserie pork on a toasted bun and red potatoes. It was so delicious and became one of my fave places to eat!!! It was almost as good as Kalua Pig from Hawaii. Inside the Ferry Building, there were Farmers Markets shops that sold many varieties of fresh vegetables, spices, fruits, flowers and many specialty restaurants that attracted many local people and workers during lunch. We went to get my fave rotisserie pork and red potatoes at least once every two weeks. Stephanie took us to the Golden Gate Bridge and thru many of the streets of hilly SFO. I will always remember Stephanie as an upbeat and wonderful friend. She was such a beautiful person that was very special to us!!!

While I worked in SFO, I became very good friends with Stefany Pikake, who originally worked at CO in Honolulu (HNL). We both worked at the Customer Service Center (CSC), and she worked in HNL with my Best Friend & longtime BFF, Yvonne D. I didn't realize there were a lot of Polynesians working for UA in SFO. Of course, I became close friends with all of them!!! Whenever I went to Hawaii, I would always spend a night in SFO to connect to Honolulu (HNL) and Stefany would pick us up and take us to eat at the Elephant Bar with my other SFO peeps Ackie, Dovalyn and Helen C.

My airline friends and my daughter, Michelle, flew to SFO to spend time with me on my days off. Angie, Nora,

Sirena & Linda W. came out to visit at different times which was very nice!!! Maggy and her two sons, Kristan & Justin and Judy C. and her daughter, Judani, flew out to visit Patricia and me. We would all go to SFO city, Chinatown and Fishermen's Wharf on BART and the Trolley and would walk around, shop & eat at Fishermen's Wharf. Linda W. and I rented a car and went to the V. Sattui Winery at St. Helena, CA. It was a nice drive there and I took a lot of pics of the Winery.

When Angie came to visit me, we went to Fishermen's Wharf to eat seafood and then to shop at the stores in SFO. Nora and Sirena came to visit, and we also went to Fishermen's Wharf to shop and eat seafood. We also went to SFO and shopped at the Westfield Mall. BART had a stop right at the Westfield Mall, San Francisco Centre, which was located two blocks from famed Union Square. BART had a Powell Street Station which was attached to the mall which had over 100 stores and the Century Theatres and three large department stores, Nordstrom, Bloomingdales and Macys. Nordstrom had two curved escalators in the center which connected to the stores in the mall. I was impressed with the Food Court located in the basement. It had a large variety of places to eat. My favorite place was the Korean Place where I would order their Barbecue Korean Short Ribs, Kal Bi!!! It came with rice, vegetables and a salad and it was a large portion. I ate there more than once and even would take a plate back to the hotel. There were also places like Charleys Philly Steak Sandwiches, Seafood Platters, Chinese, Japanese, Mexican, Vegetarian and lot of bakery and candy shops. Patricia and I were also very impressed with the Bristol Farms Grocery Market next to the Food Court. They sold my fave Poke (Raw Fish) Bowl fixed Hawaiian style, Pizza, Papaya, Prime Rib Plate Lunch with a Baked Potato, vegetables and a roll; a buffet of a variety of salads and meats, fish and chicken. Their Bakery with freshly baked rolls, bread, and cupcakes were the best!!! Our fave cupcake was Creme Brulee. We got back on BART and got off at San Bruno. We wanted to go to Lucky's Market for rocky road candy bars & groceries, Sears Mall and L & L Barbecue where we bought local plate lunches and Saimin to take back to the hotel for dinner and lunch the next day. Our hotel van would pick us up when we were ready!!!

When Angie visited, we went to another great place to eat seafood at Pier 39 Restaurant. It sat over the bay and you could watch the seals and sometimes dolphins. I would always have the Seafood Platter which had a little of everything and it was so ono (delicious). I liked the food better there than at the main Fishermen's Wharf by Alioto's. At Pier 39, we even went for a boat ride in the bay for $10.00 each person!!! When you rode the trolley to go to Fishermen's Wharf it costs 75 cents and you were given a transfer ticket. If you went to Fishermen's Wharf, ate lunch or dinner, and returned to SFO within 3 hours, you could use the transfer ticket and not have to pay to return to Westfield Mall.

Another fave area was Chinatown. I always enjoyed going there to check out the little shops with souvenirs, trinkets, jewelry, crochet runners, local markets with fresh fish, lobsters, crabs, bakeries, restaurants, and almost anything you want to see. I purchased a lot of beautiful scarfs for friends, family and myself. I even rode the cable car from SFO city to Fishermen's

Wharf. It was interesting and good to sightsee; however, it was a very rough ride…stopping and jerky. You could only buy a one-way ride. At the end of the line, you had to get off and buy a return ticket and get into the long line to get on the cable car. We rode it to Fishermen's Wharf, got on the trolley then back to Westfield Mall to get BART to return to our hotel.

I celebrated my birthday there and Patricia, Suzanne, Darlene and Tina decorated my room before I got back from work and had all my special goodies there like Rocky Road Mini Bars, a little cake and balloons and shouted, "Happy Birthday" and sang to me!!!

We loved having our friends visit us!!! My experience of working in SFO was very interesting and as I became friends with my co-workers, we started to blend our airlines together. The longer we worked there, the more we became friends, and it was more pleasant to work. A lot of resentment disappeared, and we became one airline as it was not CO vs. UA, it was becoming one UA family!!! The bottom line is we all had to work together to make UA successful and if a person couldn't adjust, that person had to make a choice to work together or quit!!! Where else could you work to get great benefits, flying privileges and an above average salary??? For me, working for the airlines was one of my three wishes and I went after that dream!!!

Patricia and I also became good friends with an employee from Houston (IAH), Suzanne P., as we worked on the same evening shift together. We all worked at the Customer Service Center (CSC), together and there was an incident when I was asked to work at the other satellite Service Center that took care of United Express Jets that flew to the smaller cities. The agents had to go and work their flights and when I looked up everyone was gone, and I was there with a large line in front of me. I called Patricia and Suzanne from the Main CSC and said I needed help. They left the other CSC and came to help me. As soon as we cleared that line, we closed that satellite CSC and went back to the main CSC. I was told whenever I worked at the satellite CSC, to ask everyone when they were leaving to work their flights and to make sure I left before everyone went to work their flights. Patricia and Suzanne were very good issuing tickets and I had retired four years before & I was asked to work in SFO so I didn't remember anything especially since I worked as the Lobby Diva in Orlando. Suzanne spent our days off together and went to SFO and Fishermen's Wharf to relax, shop and eat!!! SFO Airport also has a lot of restaurants and shops to eat. There was even an employees' diner for all the airlines employees which was very ono and very popular!!!

Our experience of working in SFO was very nice. I made many friends there and we all worked well together. One of the bad things there was the fog which usually rolled in at 7:00 pm. United Express, which flew a lot of the smaller jets to the smaller airports, were usually canceled as the visibility was Zero!!! UA didn't cover hotels due to the weather but offered discounted coupons for hotels. Suzanne, Patricia and I worked at the Customer Service Center (CSC) who helped or rebooked everyone whenever there were cancelled or delayed flights.

In August, UA Management gave us a "Going Away & Appreciation Surprise Party" at a Restaurant unknown to us

until we arrived at our destination. There were three vans that transported us there and our mystery destination was the Top of Macy's at Union Square, the Cheesecake Factory!!! First, we enjoyed Happy Hour and a great dinner including dessert and a party!!! I took a lot of pics which you can view on "My Three Wishes Fan Page." After dinner we went to a club, "The Mint" for drinks, Karaoke and Dancing. We all had a wonderful evening mingling with our Success Team and Management.

I must admit we all were very relaxed, having fun, being ourselves and were classy Party Animals!!! The last day before we flew home, we had a large sheet cake, sodas, water and got to say good-bye to everyone present in our briefing lounge.

Back to Orlando, Back to Retirement!!!

After working in SFO for 8 months, I returned to Orlando to continue my retirement years and dancing with Auntie Kau'i's group at the Polynesian Resort. I will always appreciate working in SFO, making a lot of friends there, and always fly there to connect to Hawaii. It really is true when I hear the song, "I left My Heart in San Francisco". I flew to Hawaii that December and heard that my cute friend, Stephanie G. was very ill and planned to fly back to SFO and asked Stefany Pikake if she could drive my friend, Sandy, and me to go to see Stephanie. She had lost a lot of weight but looked pretty as ever!!! I told her I came back just to see her on my way back from Hawaii!!! She was very thankful and felt very special!!! I told her she was a very special friend, and I will always remember how nice she was to Patricia and me and offered to take us around SFO!!! The next day, Stefany took my BFF Sandy and me to Fishermen's Wharf for dinner then to Union Square to watch people ice skate while we drank hot chocolate. It was very cold and we were freezing our okoles (our buns) off. Stephanie passed away a short time later and is now an angel watching over all of us!!!

I am spending a lot of time living the leisure retirement life and traveling to Hawaii and Las Vegas whenever there is a special event. Writing my book is taking a while as I have so many memories and trying to get it in chronological order. Whenever I went to Hawaii, I made sure I stopped and spent a day and night in San Francisco so that I could visit my SFO BFF Stefany Pikake. She has been a close and very dear friend of mine and we would spend the day together just hanging out and going to eat at Fishermen's Wharf or at the Elephant Bar near the airport. On one of my stopovers, Stefany drove my daughter, Michelle, and me to see my sister, Carolyn, in the hospital and my nieces, Julie, Lori and Traci in Vacaville, CA. Later, we went to Fisherman's Wharf for dinner. I will always have wonderful memories of working and making new friends in SFO. Thank you, UA, for giving me that wonderful opportunity to work there after my Retirement with CO.

Honey, I'm Home!!!

September 2012

I retired from CO with lifetime travel privileges on UA. This sounds cool and very exciting, but it isn't that easy and convenient. I get to travel space-available on any flight, anywhere UA flies. Sounds good but it takes work on my part. Work includes checking the bookings on a flight and if it looks unavailable, searching for another flight or taking a chance. Always plan to have backup plans B, C, or D to be prepared.

We are boarded by seniority and classification and hope and pray that there are enough seats to make the flight. If the flight is full, the standby list would be rolled over to the next available flight with the same destination. This could go on all day or until we made the flight. There is a price to pay for our free flying benefits. If you don't make any of the flights, your option is to get a hotel for the evening or stay at the airport gates. If the last flight was at 11:00 pm and the next flight is for 6:00 am, it wasn't worth going to the hotel as I had to be back at the airport by 4:30 am. I always got to my destination within 24 hours. I have been very lucky when I flew. I can only remember of three flights in my last 28 years that I didn't clear a flight of my choice.

I can honestly say that all the flights I was on, the flight crew was always very professional, courteous and very happy to be working their flights. The employees at the gates were always very helpful and professional. Service Directors, Helen C., and Watuma, and Miriam V., were outstanding and always very patient, courteous and helpful. Just wanted to give you a brief summary about how flying as an employee or retiree with benefits could become stressful or not. Planning, timing, and a lot of praying are the keys to getting to your destination!!!

I still entertain as a Polynesian Dancer whenever the opportunity is available. I'll be dancing as long as I can shake my booty!!! I am teaching my grand-daughters, Chelsea and Olivia, how to dance and we are currently performing as a family for "Meleilani's Polynesian Revue" with the rest of our family, dancer Michelle; drummer, Keone; and conch shell blower, Kai. Hopefully, my children will keep up with our Polynesian tradition and remember to pass this on to their children. This was the best way to bond and experience a lot of things as a family. Thank, God, for giving me the opportunities and being able to recognize it and using it wisely!!!

I had a dream, I made 3 wishes and lived my dream!!! You can be anything you want to be; you just have to be persistent and never give up on your dreams!!! If you love something that passionately, go for it and you will be successful.

Meleilani, Chelsea, Kanoe, Olivia, Michelle

Kai

Joke... the Knob

An older woman, Mrs. Jones, went to see Dr. Halstead, a plastic surgeon, and asked if he could make her look younger with a facelift. Dr. Halstead replied there is a new procedure called, "The Knob". He explained I put a knob on the back of your head and whenever you see a wrinkle, you turn the knob on the back of your head to tighten your face. It is good forever!!! Mrs. Jones agreed and had this procedure done and was happy with the results.

Ten years went by and Mrs. Jones went back to visit Dr. Halstead to ask him about the Knob. He asked her how was the Knob working out for her. She replied, it's wonderful!!! I do have a couple of questions. See those bags under my eyes, they won't go away whenever I use the Knob. Dr. Halstead examined her face and said those are not bags under your eyes. Those are your boobs!!! Oh, Mrs. Jones replied as she put her arms in the air, that explains my goatee!!!

Want some grindz (food)??? I have included a favorite recipe for you to enjoy while you relax!!!

Gau Gee

INGREDIENTS FOR A PARTY OR SMALL SERVING

Large Party	Small Party	Ingredients
2 lbs.	1/4 lb.	pork, shrimp or chicken
2 tsp	1/4 tsp	salt
4 tsp	1/2 tsp	sugar
4 tsp	1/2 tsp	cornstarch
12 tsp	1- 1/2 tsp	soy sauce (Aloha Brand)
12 tsp	1- 1/2 tsp	Bertolli extra light olive oil

Chopped up green onions or 2 slices round onion, minced

1. Mix ingredients together
2. Place about 1/4 tsp. filling on a square of Won Ton skin.
3. Moisten edges, fold Won Ton Skin in half and seal & press edges with water to look like an envelope.

Place on waxed paper to prepare it to deep fry 350 degrees. Serve with equal parts of ketchup & grape jam.

11

Celebration Of Life

On November 3, 2016, my BFFs, Meleilani and Rosana, hosted a Celebration of Life Party for me at my home. Fifty friends and families were invited. We started off with Deep Fried Gau Gee appetizers and music provided by my Cuz Al Nobriga, who flew here from Nashville, Tennessee, and my dear friends from Melbourne, Florida, Hilary and John Silva and Roland and Debbie Galindo, who provided Hawaiian music and entertainment while we ate a variety of ono delicacies. We had Pot Luck which included Spam Musubi, Broccoli Salad, Kale Salad, Pansit, Chile, Fried Chicken, Kanoe's specialties Kalua Pig, Blueberry Cream Cheese Cake and more delicacies. Our official bartender, Nilo, served his famous mojitos!!! At 4:00 pm, we put on a Polynesian Revue featuring Meleilani's Polynesian Revue featuring Meleilani, Rosana, Michelle, Chelsea, Olivia, Kai, Keone, Al Nobriga and me. The Revue included dances from Hawaii, New Zealand and Tahiti which were very colorful and upbeat!!! After the revue, I shared a picture I had taken with Ringo Starr, the Beatles, as he connected in Hawaii

from San Francisco to Australia. Hawaii local newspaper, the Honolulu Star-Advertiser, called me at home and said that Ringo Starr was having a big concert at Blaisdell Arena and they were writing a Sunday Magazine special of him and wanted to feature our picture of Kammy and me with Ringo and wanted to interview me about meeting him.

Wow, talk about finding someone from over 53 years ago especially since my name was different then. It was going to be featured two days after my celebration of life on my Mom's birthday. I also showed everyone a two-minute video of me performing my Samoan Knife Dance with a blindfold at an Orlando Night Club, Xanadu. We sat around, ate, drank and talked stories after that until 10:00 pm. It was a great celebration!!! Mahalo to Meleilani and Rosana !!! Meleilani

wanted to celebrate this now and not wait till after I passed away!!! She said that way I could enjoy it with all my friends which made a lot of sense to me!!! Among the guests that attended also were Michelle, Andy, Tyler, Chelsea & Olivia, Keone, Cathy & Kai, Hilary & John, Roland & Debbie, Jet & Kristin, Tony & Wanda, Linda & Larry, Judy & Shammon, Linda & Randy, Kanani & Jerry, Patsy & Rose, Angie & Carlos, Nilo, Franz, Patricia, Calvin, Pammy, Nikki, Marina, Moana, Gail, Andrea, Monica C., Sandy & Paul, Rosemary, Lisa, Elena, Meleilani, Rosana, and Al Nobriga.

Later that evening, Al's buddies from the Polynesian got together for a jam session here. The music was wonderful and soothing by Kaleo, Kalei, Elika and Al till about 2:00 am. This reminded me of the jam session here with Uncle Hank, Kaleo, Brown, Cuzs Gregory, Al, Imai, Rosie and the rest of Al's band Tim, Keoki and Kimo. My Cuz Al Nobriga, Keoa K. and Uncle Hank used to play in a group called The Entertainers Five in the earlier days at the Ilikai and other popular nite spots.

Hoike Hawaii usually has a competition every July at the end of the month but had to cancel this year's competition due to the Coronavirus. The Polynesian Ohanas are all sad but hope to continue this yearly event next July 2021.

A very big mahalo to Roland and Debbie & John and Hilary, and Al and my ohana for making my special day possible!!! You went up and above my expectations and I will always remember this great celebration that I could be present!!!

Meleilani and I travelled to San Francisco, Honolulu twice and Lihue, Kauai, twice on United and Hawaiian Airlines for vacation. Meleilani is a special friend and my Ohana, Michelle, Chelsea, Olivia, Keone and Kai perform in her Revues.

Kanoe's Blueberry Cheesecake

CRUST

1 1/3 Sifted Flour

1 Block Butter or Margarine

1/2 Cup Macadamian Nuts, chopped

1/4 Cup Sugar

Make Crust & Filling 24 hours ahead & Freeze

FILLING

1 - 8 oz. Philadelphia Light Cream Cheese

1 1/2 Cup Sugar

Fold in 16 oz. Whipped Real Heavy Whip Cream

1 TB. Vanilla Extract

TOPPING

1 Large Can Comstock Blueberry,

1 Packet Clear Gelatin (use to thicken Blueberry)

Refrig cake with topping 24 hrs before serving

- Bake crust at 370 degrees....15-20 min or until crust is brown

Makes (1) 9 x 12 pan ...Sheet Cake

For (2) 9 x 12 fuller pans.......Triple Filling, Double Crust & Topping

Sinful but worth it!!!

12

2019

*I*n March, Keone mentioned a 4-night cruise from Singapore (SIN) to Penang, Malaysia, and Phuket, Thailand. Michelle and I planned to go on this fabulous cruise and invited my BFFs Yvonne from Hawaii and Stefany from Vegas to go with us. The cruise was from June 3-June 7 on Royal Caribbean Cruise Lines, *Voyager of the Seas.*

I researched hotels in SIN and booked two hotels thru booking.com. We planned to go there five days before our cruise so we could enjoy the sights while we were there. It was a shame to go so far and not enjoy the city.

May was a special month for our Ohana. Two of my granddaughters were graduating. Olivia graduated from High School and Sophie graduated from College. My son, Keni, and his wife, Melissa, and their son, Maika, flew here from California, their oldest son, Brother and girlfriend, Caili, from Kona, Hawaii, their daughter, Hoku and Kalani & children, Ryder & Rayce, flew here from Colorado to help cook for Olivia's luau.

The Hawaiian food was so ono (delicious) and we also put on a Polynesian Revue featuring our Ohana (Family).

Our Cuz, Al Nobriga, who wrote, "Hele on to Kauai" flew here from Nashville and my close friends from Melbourne, Florida, Roland and Debbie G. helped to entertain with their music. The other Ohana members…Keni, Keone, Maika & Brother all helped with the tahitian drumming and Michelle, Chelsea, Olivia, Hoku, Caili and Meleilani danced and Kai blew his shell. It was a great show with our Ohana and close friends. A big mahalo to everyone that flew or drove here to make this event a big success!!! It was an event to remember!!!

Vacation Time!!!

May 29, 2019, my BFF Patricia T. picked us up at 4:30 am to drive Michelle and me to Orlando Airport. We had planned to fly out on a 6:00 am flight on UA to San Francisco (SFO) and was a little nervous flying standby as it was oversold by one. We were numbers 1 & 2 on the Standby List (S/B List) and prayed for the best. We made it on the flight and even had seats together in the Emergency Row. It was a very smooth flight, and we met my BFFs Yvonne D. and Stefany P. in SFO. Our Special Girlfriend, Service Director, Helen C. met our flight and took us to Yvonne and Stefany who were relaxing in the lounge. We relaxed and visited some of our SFO friends, Helen and Dovaney who I worked with in SFO in 2012 for eight months. We were listed in Polaris Business Class and headed to our gate. The flight was booked full in Polaris and there were only middle seats left in coach. We decided to go even if it was filling up with middle seats available. We all sat in the boarding gate area waiting to be cleared for the flight.

Good news!!! We all were seated in Polaris with separate seats and were very pleased!!! Our flight crew, under the direction of Inflight Director, Michael, was outstanding and very friendly who gave us tips and a list of places to see while we were there four days before our cruise. First let me tell you about the service in Polaris Class, which is UA's finest service. It is like dying and going to heaven!!! The seats are larger and reclines into a bed. We were given comfortable slip on slippers, a large wool blanket, and had a personal larger tv screen with awesome headphones that blows you away. I was impressed with the window. It was 11:00 am and whenever you touched it, it would get darker and looked like it was night. The flight included alcoholic or any beverage that you desired and was served with a warm selection of various nuts served in a glass cup. This is just the start of a flight that makes you feel like a very special person that you are. The following

is a menu of what was served that day which left at 11:00 am. Flight flying time was 15 hours and 20 minutes. So sit back, relax and enjoy being pampered!!!

STARTERS

Chilled Appetizer

Thai-style lemon grass shrimp, papaya salad, mango salad

SALAD

Napa cabbage, red cabbage, carrot, mango served with dressing and assorted breads

ENTREE (Your Choice of the following)

SEARED BEEF SHORT RIB

Morel sauce, stone-ground grits, green beans, roasted root vegetables

SPICY CHICKEN

Thai-style coconut-ginger broth, udon noodles

SEARED CAPE HAKE FISH FILLET

Beurre blanc, lemon risotto, baby bok choy, green beans with bell pepper and onion

INDIAN VEGETARIAN

Eggplant curry with fenugreek leaves, stir-fried carrots with coconut, spiced basmati rice with cumin seeds

DESSERTS

After your entree, enjoy any of the following:

INTERNATIONAL CHEESE ASSORTMENT

Served with grapes, crackers and port

SIGNATURE SUNDAE

Served with a choice of toppings

SWEET TREATS - Ask your Flight Attendant for today's selections.

ANYTIME A LA CARTE MENU

Indulge in mid-flight snacks any time after our dining service. Please ask your Flight Attendant for today's selections.

ARRIVAL DINING SERVICE All entrees are served with fruit, bread and dessert

FOUR CHEESE RAVIOLI

Lemon vinaigrette, yellow beets, sautéed leeks

CHINESE-STYLE PORK MEATBALLS

Ginger-garlic oyster sauce, napa cabbage, shiitake mushroom fried rice, mixed vegetables

It was a dream to sit in Polaris. It's everything you can imagine and more!!! We got to Singapore (SIN) one hour and 30 minutes before our scheduled arrival time and was happy but sad that we didn't get to enjoy our full flight time. We wanted to be pampered more!!! Michelle was disappointed because she had another movie planned before we landed.

Welcome to Singapore!!!

We lost a day flying to SIN and arrived on Thursday, May 30, 2019, and got a taxi to our hotel which was about 20 minutes from the airport. This fabulous hotel was "Village Hotel Katong by Far East Hospitality" booked thru booking.com. After searching thru many hotels, this was the best choice. The room was very large with two queen beds, lots of storage places and a large walk-in shower and dressing area. It was very clean, very quiet and we were very comfortable. After we checked in, we went to look for somewhere to eat and found a local oriental place to eat. After dinner, we went back to the hotel and walked thru the supermarket on the street level beneath the hotel. It was like going into a grocery store that carried everything from makeup, medicine, kitchen items, baby items, travel items, fresh vegetables and even a counter with fresh meat and seafood. The prices were very reasonable!!! It was like a Target or Walmart except it closed at 11:00 pm. We made reservations for the Friday Night Tour at the hotel lobby which I'll describe later.

Thursday, May 30, 2019

The next two days we had a great Buffet Brunch which featured Oriental and American Breakfast and Lunch and was included with our room. The food was very tasty with a great selection. You could even have them cook your egg in any style. The dining room was very large and comparable to a Hilton or Marriott Breakfast with more choices on the menu. We stayed in this hotel for two nites then moved to a hotel closer to the pier and the city. That afternoon we went to SIN City to shop. Stefany and Michelle got a manicure and Yvonne and I went shopping thru the local shops. We stopped at McDonalds and got something to eat. After that we were looking for the taxi sign and I was looking up and didn't realize the sidewalk had a drop and went airborne five feet in the air and landed on my face. All I remember was when I hit the concrete right on my face!!! Yvonne said she saw me go airborne and heard my forehead hit the concrete. She went down on her knees to see if I was okay and I told her I had to lay there until I got my bearings. I don't remember flying thru the air before I hit the concrete. I have a guardian angel, Pete, who took care of me.

I felt as though Pete lifted me up and put me down gently. It was a miracle because my clothes were not damaged, and my eyeglasses were not scratched. After a couple of minutes, I turned over and sat there for another minute. A nice gentleman who saw me fall helped me stand up. By some miracle, I ended up with a big egg size bump on my forehead and was able to walk across the street to get on the taxi and get back to the hotel. I was lucky that I didn't have a concussion!!! I went back to the hotel and asked the front desk to send me a bucket of ice to our room and relaxed in bed for about two hours with ice on my forehead to try to get my bump down. I didn't feel dizzy. I just wanted to lay down and relax.

We had reservations for our Night Tour and had to leave by 4:30 pm. I was not in a picture taking mood and asked my friends to please share their pics with me. We went to the Gardens by the Bay Light Show then on the bus to the Marina Bay Sands Hotel Observation Deck (56 stories via elevator) where the view of the city was gorgeous. "Crazy Rich Asians" movie featured the Marina Bay Sands Hotel in that movie. After the view, we went to the main floor of the shopping mall and walked thru the high-end mall which was beautiful!!! It was about four floors and we made our way to the boat cruise along the hotels and hi-rise buildings which were beautiful at night. We ended up at Clark Quay pronounced Clark Key known for its restaurants and bars. Michelle and I stopped by Hooters to grab a Hamburger, Fries and a drink. Yvonne and Stefany and we got separated in the mall and just met back at the hotel. The next day (Saturday), we ate a great breakfast at the hotel and got ready to move to another hotel nearer to the city and cruise port. Big mistake!!!

Saturday, June 1, 2019

We moved to Destination Singapore Beach Road Hotel which was closer to the pier and city. This hotel was not as nice as our first hotel. We got connecting rooms with two single beds in each room. The rooms were about half the size of the other hotel. No frills included no one to take our bags to our room but the nice front desk clerk offered to do that for us which we really appreciated as we had 12 bags, you know how women pack!!! A $21.00 Continental Breakfast was declined with the room rate. The nearest place to eat was across the highway. We had to use the overpass stairs to get to the street level and back to the hotel. I definitely would not recommend this hotel!!! We should have stayed in our first hotel which was much nicer and closer to everything locally!!!

That afternoon after we checked in, Yvonne, Stefany, and I went to Chinatown. We ate at a nice Chinese Restaurant at the shopping mall then I stayed at the mall while Yvonne and Stefany went to Chinatown. I didn't want to walk far as I didn't want to push it since I fell. Michelle spent the day with a high school friend, Jill, and went to eat at a market, famous for their Sweet King Crab, visited a Buddhist Temple, and went shopping. The next day, my nephew, Tim, his wife, Fang, and daughter, Annika, came to visit us from Bangkok. This was the first time I met him and he was very happy to meet our Ohana. They treated us to an oriental breakfast. His wife, Fang, is a nurse and gave me a massage to try to ease my pain from my fall. Keone, Kai, Michelle, and Tim and his family went to an island off of Singapore, Pulau Ubin, to go biking. The boat called Bumboat leaves as soon as there are 12 passengers. It leaves from Changi Point Ferry Terminal and costs $3.00 per person and less than $5.00 round trip. It is a 15-minute ride to Pulau Ubin where bikes can be rented at $8.00 usd for a leisure bike ride enjoying Tropical Birds and local stores in the Village.

Yvonne & Stefany went to the Botanical Gardens but Yvonne was very disappointed. She said the orchids in Hawaii were larger than the orchids on display. They returned to the hotel within 90 minutes. I stayed in the hotel and didn't want to take a chance to go out since it was very hot and humid. I wanted to rest before we left for our cruise the following day. I rested and watched TV and felt very relaxed and comfortable. We packed that evening as we wanted to leave the hotel by 10:30 am.

Monday, June 03, 2019

We got up early and left for the pier by taxi and got there by 10:45 am. We checked our bags then proceeded to the check-in process. We had to get copies of our passports for Phukett, Thailand, then got back into the special check in line for their Crown & Anchor Society. After checking in, we proceeded to our ship, Royal Caribbean Voyager of the Seas.

When we embarked on our cruise, our passports were taken and we were given an ID card to be used to embark, disembark the ship, for anything on the cruise as drinks, shopping items, special classes and activities, and specialty restaurants. This special ID was also our key to get into our cabin. Our credit card was part of our ID so we didn't need any cash or credit on our cruise. The night before our cruise ended, a bill was presented to us to check any extra charges. If it was okay, it would automatically get charged to our credit card. As soon as we embarked, we went to have a buffet lunch in the dining room as our rooms wouldn't be ready till after 2:00 pm.

The food was very delicious and included various selections of soups, pizzas, salads, main courses of meat, chicken and fish and a large variety of desserts. After lunch, we checked out the ship and finally got to our room at 2:00 pm. We were

very pleased with our room as we had two single beds, and a double sofa bed. I had requested a cabin with a window, and we got ceiling to floor picture windows the width of our cabin. We had lots of storage draws and two large closets and a bathroom. The two single beds were high enough to stow our suitcases under it. We were very pleased, and we were also below the top deck in front of the ship. The ship was very smooth sailing as we were not on the big ocean but sailing between the islands which made it calmer. At 4:00 pm, we had to go to a mandatory Guest Assembly Drill with our life vests to brief us where to go in case of a fire or an emergency. Our room was so nice and comfortable that we didn't have to go on the deck to see us sail as everything was seen from our large picture windows and it was air-conditioned.

We purchased the Deluxe Beverage Package which included unlimited water, various juices, coffee, tea, and virgin drinks from the bars. It was a great deal!!! The free shows included "Ice Odyssey" Ice Spectacular, Rock Rhapsody, Movies, Comedy Show of "Funny Bones", Ice Skating Sessions, and Music in Pictures Production Show starring the Royal Caribbean's Production Singers and Dancers. A Daily Planner was given out every night to let you know what activities were available the next day and the scheduled times for it. The specialty classes had a fee and there were a lot of activities going on that kept everyone busy and lots of free activities too. I missed the Flowrider and Boogie Boarding, Rock Climbing Wall Activities as an observer, and the Casino.

Some of my favorite things to observe were the Zumba Classes, the 70's Disco Inferno Street Party, Line Dance Class, and Name that Tune: Beatles Hits. There were activities going

on all day and night and it kept everyone entertained as we had 3,000 passengers. That is quite a feat to keep everyone busy and happy during the cruise. Breakfasts were served in the dining room, Cafe Promenade, or the Windjammer Cafe (Buffet Style). Lunch was served in the Windjammer Cafe (Buffet Style), and Dinners were served in the Main Dining Rooms with assigned seating, Casual Dinner in the Windjammer Cafe (Buffet Style), and Snacks were in the Windjammer Cafe 3:00 pm - 4:00 pm. The food was plentiful and very delicious!!! I gained nine pounds on our vacation trip, but it was worth it!!! It took me two weeks to lose the nine pounds when I got home!!! The best vacation is on a cruise for me!!! I loved every minute of it, and it was relaxing and wonderful!!! Cruises have always been my favorite vacations since everything is included and there is always something for everyone to enjoy!!!

Our first stop was at Penang, Malaysia. I can't tell you too much about it because I went ashore with my Family and Friends but after 1/2 hour of walking in the hot sun and humidity, I decided to return to the ship as I was getting very hot and felt like I was going to have a heat stroke. Keone and Kai walked me back to the ship and made sure I was on the ship before they returned to the rest of our party and they went shopping in a mall which they had to go by taxi. In a way, it was a good thing that I went back to the ship as a taxi only holds five passengers. I felt a lot better and explored the ship and found the Deli that was open for 24 hours with sandwiches, pizza and desserts that were complimentary. I got a sandwich and dessert and went to our cabin to eat and relax. While I was in our cabin, another smaller cruise ship sailed by and I got a picture of it!!! We could see all the islands across the straits and at night we could see all the lights from the islands. Our room had such a beautiful view with the large picture windows and I never went on deck to see that view while on the ship. We sailed from Malaysia at 10:00 pm, sailed all day at Sea and arrived at Phukett, Thailand, on Thursday at 8:00 am.

Everyone went to explore Phukett beaches and local shopping shops. Our ship didn't dock at the pier and used tenders, our lifeboats, to take the passengers to shore. I decided not to go as the beaches were about one hour to 30 minutes away and didn't feel that I could take the heat and may have to return to the ship sooner. My BFF, Yvonne, decided to stay with me and we got the tender to go to just explore the local sellers that were near the pier.

We were there for about 45 minutes then returned to the ship and enjoyed lunch and the atmosphere of the ship. Our Ohana returned to the ship and got ready for dinner in the main dining room. Dinners were always very enjoyable and our waiters from the Philippines were outstanding!!! If we couldn't decide what we wanted to choose from the dinner menu, they would suggest ordering two or more of the entrees. These were very delicious too and they didn't hesitate to get us anything we wanted including different desserts. It was so nice to be waited on!!! All of the food on the ship was very delicious and there were so many varieties…something for everyone's palate!!! After dinner, we walked around, had our mock cocktails without any alcohol also known as virgin drinks and enjoyed the activities on the ship.

On Thursday, we sailed all day and arrived at SIN at 8:00 am on Friday. We ate breakfast, our passports were returned to us, and we disembarked our ship, went thru immigration, customs and off to the airport. Keone and Kai left on their own to meet Cathy, wife and mom, as they were going to spend some time in (SIN) before returning to the U.S. The girls and I went to Singapore Changi Airport and couldn't check in for our flight until seven hours later. We immediately looked for a vendor to stow our bags so we could enjoy the airport. Changi Airport has an attached beautiful modern, air-conditioned mall with a large waterfall in the center.

The waterfall went from almost the ceiling which was about four levels to the ground level. There were a lot of different varieties of restaurants and stores that is similar to our modern shopping malls in Orlando. We spent the rest of our day shopping and went to retrieve our bags for check in 4:00 pm.

After check-in, we went to the Priority One Club which was very nice compared to United Airlines' Hemisphere Club which requires a membership. The Priority One Club was one of our benefits if you were an American Express Hilton Hotels Gold Card Holder. The club was about 3/4 full and we ate dinner there. The menu had hot soups, salads, three main entrees, varieties or rolls, desserts, juices, sodas and mixed drinks. I got to take in three guests, Michelle, Yvonne & Stefany. After dinner we just relaxed then went to the gates to board. Polaris was full and we sat in the second cabin (coach) which had extra leg room. The flight was smooth but very long!!! Michelle and I sat together and Yvonne and Stefany sat in different rows.

When we arrived in San Francisco (SFO), we all went thru Immigration and Customs very smoothly and quickly because we all had the Global Entry Card. Believe me, it is worth getting if you are flying internationally and it also includes going thru the Special TSA Pre-Check Line. Stefany got on her flight to Vegas as soon as we landed at 9:00 pm. Michelle and I planned to fly home on the 12:30 am flight from SFO to Houston (IAH) to connect to Orlando (MCO). Okay, this is the part that wasn't smooth because the SFO-IAH flight was booked so we had to spend the night in SFO. Yvonne, Michelle and I decided to spend the night in the airport. We found some nice lounge chairs to get to sleep and this also helped us with the hassle of the long check in lines in the morning and our first Orlando (MCO) flight left at 8:00 am so it was not worth it to rent a hotel room and stay in it for about four hours then return to the airport. Sad news, our Plan B didn't work so we tried for the two flights later and both were booked. Our good friend, Service Director, Helen, was working and told us to just try for the 3:00 pm non-stop to Orlando which we did make. Yvonne got on her flight about 11:00 am to Honolulu (HNL). So, flying stand-by is not always that easy but we were happy to use our flying benefits and wait as long as we got home!!! I decided I did not want to fly on any long flights over 10 hours in the future!!! It is not fun sitting on a long flight with a bad back!!! We all got home safely and rested for about a week before we felt back to normal from the jet lag.

On Monday, June 10, 2019, I went to the Emergency Room at Dr. Phillips to get my head checked for a concussion from my fall in Singapore (SIN). I was lucky, I didn't have a concussion. The following week, I had a lump on my forehead that wouldn't go away. I went to check it out with my dermatologist, and he scheduled me for surgery the following week. I was lucky that he cut through a crease on my forehead and it didn't leave a scar. It was benign and turned out to be an ingrown hair that got infected where I fell on my forehead. I feel that my guardian angels, my Ma and Pete Camacho, are always watching over me. The rest of 2019 was nice for me without any more drama!!!

Corn Souffle

1 cup of sour cream (8 oz)

2 eggs, beaten

1 stick of butter

1 can whole corn - 15.25 oz size with juice

1 can cream corn

Fried chopped sweet onions to taste

1 box of jiffy corn muffin mix

- Add (1) box frozen chopped spinach or broccoli (creative & ono, optional)
- Mix sour cream, eggs & butter
- Pour corn into mix…mix well
- Add onions & corn mix
- Bake at 350 degrees for 45 min

Thank you, Sarah, for sharing!!!

13

2020: Coronavirus

Today, March 20, 2020, marks a new day in history in Orlando, Florida. Coronavirus, (COVID-19) is spreading and is affecting many countries all over the world. It started in Wuhan, China, and is affecting China, Korea, Italy and a lot of European and Asian countries. It has been spreading like wild-fire and is similar to the flu except worse. It didn't take long to work its way to the United States (USA) as it is believed to have entered the USA from tourists and returning residents. It attacks your lungs and a lot of people with weak immune systems mainly get pneumonia and pass away. This includes anyone who has an illness that lowers any resistance to protect us as asthma, diabetes, treated with chemotherapy, pneumonia, etc. This Coronavirus has changed the world and is easily spread from anyone traveling with symptoms that is not noticeable until it is too late. There is a 14-day incubation period before anyone realizes that and shows any symptoms. These people could be "carriers" of COVID-19 and do not know that they are spreading it.

It's hard to believe that Michelle, Yvonne and I had planned to fly to Milan about three weeks before and planned to go to visit Venice, various small towns of Italy, Germany, France and end up in Geneva, Switzerland to visit my grand-daughter, Sophie.

March 23 - all the State Parks and Beaches in Florida were closed to cars driving and parking on the beaches. The people could still walk on the beaches but have to keep their groups of people to 10 or less and distance 6 feet away from other people.

The news of COVID-19 started a week before we planned to leave, and we decided not to take a chance of getting stranded in Europe. Luckily for us, I didn't make any hotel reservations as the dates I requested were not available, so we didn't know what cities we were visiting and in what order. We were going to just plan our itinerary whenever we arrived. We had a pretty good idea of where we wanted to visit. It was going to be an adventure. We were planning to visit Sophie in Geneva and be a tourist there. The only thing we had planned was the day to fly over to Milan, Italy, and return via Geneva a week later. We were all excited to go on our trip but faced the reality of getting stranded there and also getting sick. We didn't know it was going to be a worldwide virus that was spreading so quickly and so many people were dying from this.

Disney World and Universal Studios were closed until further notice followed by all Disney and Universal Hotels, restaurants and shops. Sea World, Legoland and Gatorland followed. It was originally going to be for two weeks then changed to close until further notice.

March 24 - My grandson, Kai, and I went to Publix to take advantage of Senior Shopping Hours on Tuesdays and Wednesdays from 8:00 am to 9:00 am. Lucky for me, there wasn't a crowd there. I only bought orange juice there and two gallons of spring water. We went to Target after that with less than 20 people in the store. I hit the jackpot there!!! I found toilet paper, paper towels, paper napkins, Lysol Spray, Clorox bleach, and Seventh Generation Disinfecting Wipes. Everything was limited to (1) item per customer. I also got Zephyrhills gallon spring water limited to (2) per person. They allowed me to purchase double of each since Kai was with me. What I don't understand is there is a shortage of toilet paper. All the stores seem to be out of toilet paper. The shortage is also in Honolulu. Hopefully, I have enough for six weeks.

March 29 – There are only certain essential stores open like grocery stores, pharmacies, medical facilities, gas stations, hospitals, fast food and order for take-out or pick up from restaurants. Everything on TV is about COVID-19. I know it's to keep everyone informed but thank, God, we can turn it off or change it to another channel. It is very depressing. We are constantly reminded of the statistics. I refuse to listen to this depressing news all day and decided to watch stress-free programs. Remember I don't like stress especially if I can't control it!!!

I surf the channels, check all the good movies and record it so I can watch it at my convenience. Movies make me relax and make me happy. Being retired, the only stress in my life is watching my fave soaps, Young and the Restless and The Bold and the Beautiful. Unexpected necessary bills like damage from a storm, hurricane, leaking roof, car repairs and anything out of the ordinary throws everything off but I have to find a way to repair and pay for these unexpected expenses. So, if everything goes smoothly, I am fine and don't have any stress.

Sometimes too much information (TMI) can make us more stressful!!! Of course, we care about the updates but give me a break!!! All the networks are carrying the same information as the President and Governor of Florida with the same speech being covered on NBC, CBS and ABC. We are being over-saturated with the updates that I'd rather not watch or listen to it as it will be summarized on the evening news. I personally feel that the only way to control this is to shut everything down for one month without exceptions similar to "Martial Law" and tell everyone to be prepared for it by buying enough groceries and essentials to last for a month. It will be difficult to do but we have to prevent it from spreading. This is just my personal opinion and don't care to go into any more about COVID-19 as anyone can check its progress in the USA and form your own opinion. Let's shut the USA down then come back stronger and healthier. Unless this happens, things will never be the same!!!

There was a situation that happened to me. I decided to go to a fast-food restaurant to buy something for dinner. Everyone is opened for order online and either pick up or drive thru or have it delivered. I walked into this restaurant and went up to the counter and was not helped for two minutes. Finally, the drive thru cashier asked me if I was helped yet. I said no and she told me I had to order from the kiosk. The screen was nasty!!! Covid-19 could be spread by the screens on the kiosks. Everyone was so afraid of these machines or kiosks replacing the workers giving personal customer service. This is the time to help the customers and give them customer service!!! Cover those kiosks until this is over, have antibacterial wipes next to these nasty screens and assist the customers with their orders. I will never go back to that restaurant again. There were more workers there and I was the only customer. No eating in was allowed-only take out-in the restaurant. Things definitely will change how we do things. We are so spoiled compared to other countries and we forget how good we have it in America and will definitely see the changes in the future. The kiosks in the grocery stores, department stores, airports, restaurants should have antibacterial wipes near it and customer service personnel to assist the customers or the wipes will disappear as there is already a shortage of wipes now. Those screens are nasty and shouldn't be used by the public. Good way to spread coronavirus!!! Again, this is only my opinion and we will have to adjust when the changes are here. I have to give Target, Publix Market, Walmart, Sam's, and also Costco kudos for doing a good job of having their employees wipe down the carts and getting clean ones as you enter, wipe down the check-out kiosks and stations for self-check-out and always having personnel to assist you when you check out!!! Okay, enough about COVID-19. This is a big part of history and you can research it as it will be a very important part of our history. It is very serious so you can research it for more information. I am falling asleep and have to take a nap. I'll continue this later!!!

April 3 - Went to walk in for my doctor without an appointment. Things are different now. I gave them my

symptoms and they explained what I had to do. I was given an appointment time and instructions on how to log in on my phone and my doctor would call me at 10:45 am and our visit would be via cell phone for a televisit. I came home and ate breakfast then went thru the steps of logging in. I hate to type on my cell because my fingers always overlap the squares. Thank, God, I had an hour and 30 minutes to do this before my appointment. It wasn't that difficult to log in and I was ready for my call at 10:45 am. After our Televisit, my doctor told me to call her if I got a fever, but my symptoms didn't sound like Coronavirus. She told me to stay at home and don't go out!!! What would I do if I had an ear infection??? How could she examine me??? I guess I would have to go to the emergency room to be checked physically!!! These were just questions I wondered about if I really needed to be physically checked.

Enough said about the Coronavirus. It is not going away anytime soon!!! The Mayor issued that everyone that is in a public place should be wearing a face mask to help prevent the spread of this virus. I, personally, hate to wear a mask as it is hot and difficult to breathe. This gives me the incentive to stay at home more and work on my book and finish doing things around here like getting rid of things I don't need. Time to take a break and then start of something fresh!!! Decisions, decisions!!!

Vacation in Hawaii (Joke!!!)

A couple visiting Hawaii was walking in Waikiki and stopped a local guy, Kimo, (originally from Belgium) and asked him, "Sir, what is the correct way to say Waikiki??? Is it pronounced Waikiki or Vaikiki??? Kimo answered, It's Vaikiki!!! The couple said thank you very much and Kimo replied, "You're Velcome!!!"

Time to go to the Lua (Toilet), wash your hands and check out this recipe!!!

Kanoe's Hamburger Dip

2 lbs. Hamburger

1 lb. Velveeta Cheese (Mexican)

1 Sweet Round Onion

4 cups or 2 small bottles
Chunky Picante Salsa Sauce

- Fry Hamburger till well done
- Add chopped Sweet Onion
- Add Chunky Picante Salsa Sauce
- Add Velveeta Cheese (Mexican)
- Let boil then simmer for 3 hours on very low or warm heat
- Sprinkle chopped green onion on dip & serve hot
- Serve with taco chips

This can be frozen then reheated in the microwave to eat.
Very ono!!! (delicious)

Lumpia

2 lb. Ground Beef or Pork

1/4 cup Carrots (Sliced)

5 pc. Garlic (Diced)

1/2 cup Green Onion (Sliced)

1/2 cup Sweet Round Onion (Diced)

1 can Sliced Water Chestnuts

3 bags Bean Sprouts

4 oz. Panda Oyster Sauce

2 pkg. Square Lumpia Wrap

- Brown Beef or Pork & season & add Oyster Sauce
- Add Garlic & onion (Saute)
- Add Vegetables & drain & cool
- Wrap ingredients in Lumpia Wrap
- Bowl of 1/2 cup water & 1 TB cornstarch to seal
- Deep fry till golden brown 375 degrees

14

Special Friends

Fabulous Four (Fab Four)
(Sassy Gals with Class)

- *NORA...* (Puerto Rican)

  My closest friend and best roommate at CO, shared the same birthday together. Beautiful model, actress, awesome personality & fun. Retired from CO & currently a Flight Attendant for another major airline.

- *CATHY...* (Haole)

  Daughter-in-law, beautiful blonde with a positive attitude & Flight Attendant for a major airline. Cast actress for Universal's Halloween Horror Nights & Mardi Gras.

- *ANGIE...* (Mexican)

  Beautiful green eyes with dark hair Biach, great personality, smart, sassy, fun, close friend, co-worker at CO and now at WDW and loves ColorStreet. Youngest FAB FOUR.

- *KANOE...* (Hawaiian) Loves to dance, Polynesian Dancer, Retired from CO, Loves to host Parties at home. All of the above and more!!!

- *JUDY...* (Jamaican Princess) (Our Plus One)

  Beautiful smile, smart, great personality, awesome Karaoke Queen that owns the mike at parties and loves to dance!!! Hangs with us whenever she can!!!

Co-Party Animals

Our special Party Animals included Nora, Judy C., Maggie, Angie, Nilsa, Nilo, Miguel, Lisa, Thalia, Sharie, Chris, Angel, Shauna, Tom, Karen, Brett, Patsy, Andrea, Cathy, Keone, John and me. These were our Pleasure Island Dance Dream Team that loved to dance, drink socially and dine!!! This also included Delta and GOAA (Orlando International Airport) friends!!! These Party Animals were at all my parties at my home and Rocked the Parties!!!

YVONNE D... (BFF) my very best friend since we met at the University of Hawaii, and calabash sista for over 62 years. Later we worked at Hawaiian Telephone Company together for seven years. Our desks faced each other in our large business office, and we went on breaks and lunch together and we even got pregnant about the same time with six other women in our office. She used to go to watch my Polynesian Revue at Fort DeRussey and even helped me pick out the different props for the revue. On weekends, we went to see Don Ho and other shows in Waikiki. Yvonne, Freddie and I also went to the Merry Monarch, the Peppermint Lounge, the Three Amigos Show, and K. C. Drive Inn for Saimin and their specialty Waffle Hot Dogs. I left Hawaii in 1967 and moved to California and later Yvonne got hired by Continental Airlines. Whenever I went home to Hawaii, we would always spend time together. We would always go out to Ala Moana Shopping Center, go to a Korean Restaurant to eat Bulgogi and Kim Chee Plate Lunch, go to eat at a Chinese Restaurant downtown Honolulu at Chinatown and also go to a Hawaiian Restaurant to eat Hawaiian Food like Kalua Pig, Poi, LauLau, Lomi Salmon, Chicken Long Rice and Haupia (Coconut Pudding). Most of the recipes are in this book. Seek and you shall find!!!

We travelled to Beijing, China, for a shopping and sightseeing trip and especially remember going to see the Great Wall of China and lost my good prescription eyeglasses there. We found a lot of bargains at the Silk Market in Beijing. I purchased a full-length black heavily lined suede coat which they tried to sell me for $135.00 and I bargained until I got it for $35.00. I also bought a Samsonite carryon bag for $25.00 and jade and pearl jewelry. Yvonne couldn't believe I got my coat for $35.00 and the next day we went back to the Silk Market and I got Yvonne a brown coat like mine for $35.00 also. I am Chinese and got lucky with my bargaining. Last year, we went on a trip to Singapore with my daughter, Michelle, and another BFF, Stefany P. as described in my Singapore chapter. This year Yvonne, Michelle and I had planned to fly to Milan, visit Venice and different towns on Italy's coasts, Germany, France and end up in Switzerland to visit my granddaughter, Sophie. Our plans were abruptly changed because of the Coronavirus. Yvonne has been a great friend and we are on the phone at least 3 times a week between 2-4 hours. She has helped me proofread and give me ideas about our past.

LIZ T... I will never forget how special she is. Liz has done so many special things for me. A co-worker asked me to travel to Spain for 4 days. I asked her if I could invite Liz since she could help us translate. Two days before our trip, my coworker cancelled because she was sick. Good thing I invited Liz or I wouldn't have gone by myself. Steve, a pilot friend from CO, saw us at Newark (EWR) Airport and asked us where we were flying. We said Madrid. Steve said that he was sure John, Karen L.'s brother, was flying that trip. Karen is a co-worker from Orlando. Steve went to look for John to let him know that Liz and I were going to be on his flight. During our flight, we spoke briefly with John and he got permission from the Captain for us to ride in the crew van to their hotel where we hopefully could book a room. After we arrived at the hotel, John told Liz and me to meet him, and the other two captains on our flight, at 5:00 pm and they would show us around, go out to dinner and go bar hopping. We rode the train to get to a plaza there where we had dinner, went to the Mushroom Bar and then back to the hotel by 11:00 pm as they needed so many hours rest before flying out the next day. We were there on a holiday weekend and most of the stores were closed. I learned never to travel during a holiday after that.

Another trip, I was going to Costa Rica with my BFF Ada for an event and she couldn't go at the last minute. I had intended to go by myself and Liz asked me who I was going with and I said myself. Liz said no, I will go with you. Thank, God, as the main language there is Spanish. Liz accompanied me there and got me settled in and flew back the next day. What a sweetheart, Liz was my interpreter and I got to be with other English-speaking friends. Liz and I had also been on other trips together to Las Vegas for the Consumers Electronic Shows (CES), San Francisco (SFO) for Continental Baggage Training and leisure trips to Hawaii. My grandson, Tyler, was having a barbecue birthday party and Liz offered to barbecue chicken which she brought over in her special sauce and had to leave early for another event. Honestly, could you ever have such a beautiful, loving person who is that special??? I am lucky to have her as a friend!!! Later I decided to tile my home and Liz also helped me pick out the tile for my home when I had the carpet replaced from my foyer, hallway, the laundry room and my kitchen. I asked her recommendation since her home has beautiful tile floors. She actually took me to the tile outlet and helped me select the tile from the different styles to make sure it wasn't slippery for future falls. I had the tile delivered and we got the installer to do the job a week later. The day of installation, we were short (2) boxes of tile. I called Liz and asked her if she could pick up (2) boxes of tile and bring it to my home and she dropped everything she was doing and did this for me!!! I have a lot of great BFF gals and Liz was always there for me whenever I needed her never expecting anything in return!!! There are not too many friends that are special, available and giving like Liz. Thank you, Liz, you will always be special to me!!!

BOOBIE LISA... Boobie is also one of my special BFFs. We took several trips to Las Vegas to the Consumers Electronic Shows, (CES); Honolulu, Oahu; Kona, Hawaii; and Lihue, Kauai. I always called her my "Body Guard" when we went night clubbing because I am short and petite and everyone would bump into me on the crowded dance floor and Boobie would switch places with me so that the people couldn't bump into me. Boobie was fun at work also and an outstanding ticket agent at CO and worked with a lot of speed. When my boyfriend, Pete C., passed away in my home, Boobie came to my home and spent the afternoon with me on her day off. She also accompanied me to Honolulu for Pete's memorial services. Pete was like a big brother to her. Boobie and a group of Continental friends went to Disney's Pleasure Island every Tuesday night and we could go to all the clubs for $6.00 a person with our CO ID. Our favorite club was 8-Trax that played 70's Disco Music. We would all meet there and go club hopping. Boobie and I also traveled to Hawaii every year for the Aloha Week Hoolaulea, an event where the main street in Waikiki, Kalakaua, was shut down and floats with entertainment and all kinds of food and local souvenirs as flower leis, shell leis, items made from Koa and drinks and a variety of plate lunches were sold. Local entertainment performed on the floats from 7 pm until 11 pm. It was great!!! It was the same Hoolaulea event that my Polynesian Revue entertained in 1962. Boobie and I also traveled to Kona, Hawaii, to visit my son, Keni and his family. Boobie and I travelled to Las Vegas for the Consumers Electronics Show (CES) from 2002 until 2008. It was a very special event where all the latest electronics were displayed and demonstrated for the upcoming 6 months. That was always a great event to attend and usually was attended by 160,000 people from all over the world. It was very crowded!!! We felt very special to go to it as company reps had to be invited to attend and no one could just go there. We had a lot of fun attending that every year!!! The first year that I attended CES in Vegas in February 2002, I won the second grand prize drawing of a Mitsubishi High Definition Digital Video Cassette Recorder (VCR) which was not even in the stores yet. I asked my electronics store, Sound Advice, if they had one on display and the salesman told me that it was coming out in 6 months. He was surprised when I told him that I won it at CES. I felt very special!!! I was notified that I won the VCR while I was still in Vegas and asked them to ship it to me which I got within 30 days. Would you believe, I still have it!!!

ADA T... another good friend of mine who transferred from Continental Airlines (CO) Reservations Tampa (TPA) to Orlando (MCO). There were 17 people who transferred in. Ada and I became very good friends. I was the Trainer at MCO and Ada became an Airport Ticket Agent. We used to travel a lot and she attended my Hawaii high school reunions in Las Vegas and my classmates loved her so much that they made her an honorary class member. We also travelled to Costa Rica and Hawaii together. Ada loved being part of my Ohana (family) and we had a great time together. Ada was my most kolohe (rascal) BFF. After my BFF Pete Camacho passed away a year before, I decided to date younger guys. I didn't want to lose anyone older again. Ada convinced me that it was okay to date someone younger than me and I became a Cougar!!! Now that I am older, I decided I am a Jaguar, but you can call me JAG. Ada was my Kolohe girlfriend and we became very mischievous at times in a good, fun-loving way!!! Ada gradually transferred back to TPA where she owned a home and retired and moved to Reno to be near her daughter and family!!!

NORA G… my very sweet and best roommate that stayed with me two nights a week and lived in Sarasota with her family. CO closed Sarasota and Nora commuted to Orlando which was about two hours each way just to continue working for CO. We became very good friends when we were talking at the Ticket Counter and found out that we had the same birthdays. I was having a July 4th Party at my home and asked her if she was going to come to the party and Nora said she would and celebrate her birthday early. I asked her when was her birthday and when she said July 7, I told her no way!!! That was my birthday too!!! We became instant BFFs and got along really well. Nora is the best roommate a person could ask for!!! I never thought I would like anyone staying with me, but Nora and I hit it off mainly because we have the same birthdays and similar personalities. Nora worked here for three days a week and stayed with me two nights a week. She is the sweetest, very giving person who expected nothing in return for all the nice things she did for me. Actually, Nora spoiled me rotten!!! It was nice to have her as a roommate as we went out dancing at Pleasure Island with Boobie, Angie, Nilo and the rest of our CO co-workers. She would also call me during her break at work and say want to go to a movie tonight or out for a snack, come home and change and we were on the move and met other co-workers. I loved having her stay with me until I was offered an opportunity to go to SFO to train the UA agents there for CO's computer system since CO and UA merged. I went to work in SFO from January till August 2012 and Nora stayed with our good friend, Judy C., until Nora retired before I returned to Orlando. Nora and I used to go to Red Coconut at Universal City Walk with our other BFFs Angie and Cathy!!! Those were the good 'ole days!!! Some nights we were joined by Judy C., and Maggy K.!!! I miss those days!!! Red Coconut had a live band that played music from the 50's till 2020!!! Herb Williams had the best band there and we loved dancing to their music!!! We would then go dancing at the other clubs there. Nora had a big birthday party on July 7, 2007, and got me a special birthday cake of my own!!! That was a surprise and very thoughtful of her. Nora's 07-07-07 Birthday Party was an elaborate costume party, and everyone looked so elegant especially Nora in her fitted gold finger body suit. Nora is a very special person and friend, and I enjoyed her living with me!!! Nora is retired and now working for another major airline!!!

PATRICIA T… another BFF and my most serious best friend. She would treat me like her daughter sometimes. I could never talk about my boyfriend with her as she would give me that "eye", you know that look that parents give us!!! Patricia was one of our Red Coats at CO and was very strict and firm at work with everyone. No one messed with her!!! Patricia and I went to Hawaii several times, Beijing and Shanghai, China, and Las Vegas.

We also worked together in SFO from January to August 2012. We are both retired now and still hang out together and live five minutes away from each other. Whenever I travelled to Hawaii, Las Vegas and Singapore, Patricia would take my daughter, Michelle, and me to the airport at 4:45 am several times. Talk about a good friend!!! She is a sweetheart!!! She would also pick me up at the airport if she was available whenever I came home. Patricia has even taken me to the Emergency Room when I had to be driven there!!! She is a very good friend but very strict and would give me a lecture sometimes so I would be very selective on the subjects I would discuss with her!!! Whenever she got out of hand, I did let her know that I was an adult and not her child, and older than her!!! Patricia was a very close friend of Pete & spent the day with me the day Pete had a heart attack and passed away at my home!!! CO's Supe, Leon J., drove Patricia to my home to be with me for the day. Patricia's daughter, De Licia, also stayed with me for moral support. Today Patricia and I are just enjoying being retired and relaxing at home. We live five minutes apart and get to do things together if it's before 5:00 pm as we both don't like to drive in the evening!!!

LORETTA P... A special thanks to her for spending the night with me when Pete passed away and for taking me to the airport to fly to Hawaii. Lo Parker came here with her two-year-old daughter, Nicole, which I will always remember and be thankful!!!

> ★ *My definition of retirement is having a lot of time to do the things that I have been trying to do for years but don't want to do!!!* ★

⋆ Procrastination… Delaying things that I have been trying
to do but get easily distracted ⋆

NILO E… has always been special!!! He was a hard-working team member that was very polite, knowledgeable, speedy and courteous at CO or anytime we were together!!! Nilo used to make us Cuban Coffee, "CAFESITO CUBANO", for our break at the Ticket Counter whenever we were not busy. Nilo used to be my DJ at all my parties. He would make the best mojitos and bring his ice chest with everything he needed for his popular mojitos and also bring his boom box and cds to fill the latin/disco atmosphere on my back lanai by the pool. We even had a night club effect with a bar and the disco lights pulsing to the music cranked up. My parties had something for everyone. My family room had Karaoke with friendly challenges since the Karaoke would score points at the end of the song. Everyone tried to beat each other's' scores which was 100 if you were perfect!!! At 10 pm, Michelle and I would put on a mini Polynesian show (about 20 minutes) which included black lights and audience participation. After the show, we continued to eat, drink and dance!!! Curfew time was 2:00 am so I would shut down the lanai at 1:15 am and bring the party in the house. Trust me, the music was cranked out loud and the neighbors were always invited. My parties were very popular and well-known at the airport and I have had many!!! The word got around and everyone was invited!!! The largest group here was 150 people at one of my parties. Some of the parties included an annual Halloween Party, New Years' Eve Party, Birthday

Parties and my Retirement Party!!! I enjoyed hosting these parties and I had the best party house with entertainment!!!

Everyone had to remove their shoes as they entered, a Hawaiian custom, and I always told everyone to enjoy themselves. My home is like a buffet. You can enjoy it while you are here; however, you are not allowed to remove or take anything when you leave except the booze you brought or any food!!! Since I retired, I don't have any parties anymore because I now have a white carpet in my family room!!!

Auntie Kau'i and the Polynesian Resort

Auntie Kau'i was a beautiful, Polynesian Wahine (Woman) that was so full of energy, loved to dance the hula and shared all of her talent with the wahines and kanes (men) who wanted to learn our beautiful Polynesian dances and culture. Auntie Kau'i was an Ambassador at the Polynesian Resort who used to sew leis, entertain the guests and spread the Aloha spirit!!! Auntie Kau'i, Ku'ulei and Brian, all Polynesian Ambassadors, used to sit at the welcome area surrounded by beautiful flowers where they sewed leis for the guests as you entered into the resort and would talk story with the guests. The leis and flowers were for the hair and wrists for wahines (women) and keikis (children). Our Ohana (family) moved to Orlando in June 1974 and went to the Polynesian Luau at Disney where I met Auntie Kau'i who was the Mistress-of-Ceremonies (MC) and in charge of the revue. We loved the revue and was excited to attend the luau and ate the polynesian delicacies. I used to see Auntie Kau'i whenever we had dinner at the Polynesian Resort and finally joined her halau (dancers) in 2008 whenever I retired from Continental Airlines. It was nice to dance with her as she taught the traditional hulas and my revues were more modern with dances from Hawaii, Samoa, Tahiti, New Zealand, Guam, Japan and seasonal holiday dances. 1962 was the last time I had taken lessons and learned everything from Johnny Watkins and had used his style of dancing in my revue. He was my favorite Kumu and Auntie Kau'i was also a favorite Kumu of mine. Auntie Kau'i was very laid back and taught us how to dance with the employees of the Polynesian Resort. She was always very happy, made sure we danced well and also very firm. She whacked us with the puili (split bamboo) if anyone made a mistake to make us aware to be serious and pay attention!!! She was so full of the aloha spirit and taught us well. She would get us ready to compete in the Hoike Hawaii every July. Auntie Kau'i and I had a special bond as we were both raised in Honolulu, Hawaii, and were children during the bombing of Pearl Harbor, World War II. We used to talk story about our hana butta days when we were growing up in Honolulu. We talked about how we lived through the different changes as we grew up. The days when we all used to keep our home doors unlocked, no cell phones, we played outside and listened to the Long Ranger, the Shadow Knows, Gene Autrey, etc., as TV was not even invented at that time. We all had to be home before dark and our families always ate dinner together. Our parents were very strict with us and all they had to do was to give us the "stink eye" which meant don't even try it or you are going to get lickin!!! I watched a local show the other night and the guys talked about how our parents would hit us whenever we did anything wrong and we always listened to them or be in trouble. The guys on TV said now the kids threaten to call the DCF (Department of Children and Family) when you try to discipline them. In our days that would be called attempted murder if they did that now. Actually, I have to say my favorite Kumus in my lifetime were John Piilani Watkins, Honolulu, Hawaii and Auntie Kau'i Brandt, Orlando, Florida. Ku'ulei was also my very favorite hula instructor from Orlando. Ku'ulei's body and hands were so graceful, her choreography and her moves flow with the music with a lot of feelings and a touch of class. Auntie Kau'i was a very special friend and Kumu Hula

The17th Annual Ho'ike Hawai'i Event
July 19-20, 2014 in Orlando

*i*CFLORIDA.com

Instructor who I became friends with from 2008-2020. After I retired from Continental Airlines in 2008, I joined her Halau (hula class). She was the sweetest and funniest person full of energy, loved and admired by everyone. Her Halau won First Place in the Wahines' Division at Ho'ike Hawai'i 14th Annual Hula Competition at the Wyndham Hotel in Orlando in July 2011. We wore beautiful purple holomus, draped with white shell leis, white pearl earrings, and purple and white flowers in our hair. We danced to the song, Mi Nei, (How about me???) to the lovely sounds and voices of Kaleo, Lopaka, and friends as Auntie Kau'i interpreted this beautiful and sexy Hawaiian hula!!! Our hula was graceful, and we floated across the stage with class and grace!!! We captivated the audience's attention and pleased the judges. We Rocked!!! Other events that stand out was Hoike 2014.

My daughter, Michelle, won First Place, using the Poi Balls in a Maori Dance representing New Zealand.

We danced "Ha'a Hula" before the trophies were awarded featuring Auntie Kau'i, surrounded by the beautiful rainbow colored holomus worn by Kanoe, Michelle, Kanani and Meleilani and other ladies, wore white and purple holomus. My Cuz, Al Nobriga, who wrote the very popular, "Hele On To Kauai" and his group from Hawaii and Nashville, included my Cuz Imai, Cuz Greg, Tim, Kimo and Keoki, were the opening act for the featured group, Maunalua, from Hawaii. It was a great show!!! The next day, Al and group including Uncle Hank all came to my home for a jam session!!! Reminded me of the good 'ole days in Hawaii. My other Cuz, Rosie, flew in from California to join us that weekend. Whenever Al comes to visit me from Nashville, we always call his musician friends to come here to jam and it is nice just sitting around and listening to the musical sounds of the guys. We have had Uncle Hank, Kalei, Brown, Kaleo and Elika jam here just singing the real 'ole Hawaiian songs. It reminded me of our Ohana that used to go to the beach every weekend for a pot-luck picnic. Us kids used to run in the park or go swimming with some adults and the rest of the Ohana just jammed with their ukes, guitars, and singing. Our Ohanas were all musicians and dancers who entertained professionally!!! During the month of February 2020, Auntie Kau'i and Pono, were called back home and now are angels that watch over us. Auntie Kau'i will always be remembered by everyone as being a beautiful Kumu and very special friend that everyone loved and admired!!!

Pete's Portuguese Bean Soup

4 Smoked Ham Hocks

1 Clove Garlic

2 Bay Leaves

1 lb. Steak or Ham(cubed) (optional)

1 can Tomato Sauce, Garlic

2 cans Kidney Beans (15.5 oz ea)

2 cups Carrots, 1 Sweet Onion

6 Baby Red Potatoes (sliced half)

3 cups Cabbage, chopped

1/2 box or 3/4 cup Elbow Macaroni

1/2 Portuguese Sausage, sliced

- Boil ham hocks and drain once to lessen salty taste (about 2 hours) till tender
- Add 3 cups hot water with 1 & 1/2 tsp. Knorr Chicken Flavor Bouillon & boil
- Add as needed (1 cup hot water with 1/2 tsp Bouillon mix)
- Add all vegetables, chopped sweet onion & Garlic Tomato Sauce.
- Cook until tender.
- Add macaroni (10 min) before done.

- Add Cabbage & Portuguese Sausage

This is my best friend's recipe!!! Pete loved to cook and was an outstanding chef!!!

Pete is now my Guardian Angel watching over us & flying with the angels!!!

15

Funny Memories, Bits & Pieces

Jury Duty

$\mathcal{E}$veryone hates jury duty, and I am no exception. I tried to think of ways I could get out of jury duty but couldn't so I reported like I was assigned. The day before I was scheduled, I had to call in and a recording would let me know if I was one of the lucky chosen jurors. I sat in a large room and made sure I had things to keep me entertained until my number was called. Our group that was selected were told to go have lunch and we would be assigned to a court case at 1:00 pm.

After lunch we were assigned to a room where we would leave our personal belongings. We finally were called into a court room and we all sat down. The judge said everyone please return to the waiting room except Miss Kaye, which was me. I had all kinds of things going thru my head like what did I do, am I in trouble??? The judge asked me if I knew anyone sitting in the court room and I looked around and didn't recognize anyone. The arresting officer said you work with my wife. I said who is your wife??? He said Riema. I looked at the officer as I pointed to him and said Jeff??? You look good!!! I hadn't seen Jeff for awhile in his uniform and didn't recognize him. The last time I saw Jeff & Riema, they came to my Halloween Party in costumes. Riema was dressed as Dracula and Jeff was dressed in drag as a "She Devil" in a long, flowing, bright red gown and long wig with his beard!!! Would you believe I was kicked out as a juror??? I couldn't go back to the juror room and had to exit the court room, and someone had to bring my personal things to me in the hall. Wow, what just happened??? Whew!!! I called my Supervisor Rick to tell him what happened and we both laughed about it!!!

Childhood Memories

Children are born without prejudice and hate. I don't remember growing up that way as Hawaii is a melting pot of all nationalities and Polynesians are very loving and giving people!!! I had a happy childhood and wasn't around bullying. It's sad that children and adults are exposed to that today. We are all human beings. No one should feel superior to anyone. Everyone should try to help people and not put them down. I notice that some people who are insecure treat others badly by bullying other people and trying to feel superior. It doesn't cost anything to be kind to anyone.

★ Be careful of the toes you step on!!! One day you may have to kiss the okole (ass) that is attached to those toes!!! ★

Be Confident and Believe in Yourself!!!

When I was entertaining, I bid on a show for a luau. During my interview, the Manager of the Officers' Club said to me, your competitor bid $100.00 under you. Without missing a beat, I replied, "Do you want Steak or Hamburger???" I was hired and continued doing all the military clubs after that!!!

After I was hired by Eastern Airlines, I dissolved the Micronesian Revue because I knew I wouldn't be able to get weekends off to do shows. The General Manager of the Officers' Club called and asked me to do a luau and I told him that I wasn't entertaining anymore because of my employment with Eastern. He asked me to please do this for him as he was retiring after this luau. We did this for him as he treated our group well and we entertained for the past four years at the military clubs. This was our last Revue.

Lessons for the Future

TILE FLOORS .... are beautiful!!! It is very hard on your feet, knees and your back. You should wear padded shoes or slippers on tile and terrazzo floors!!! Walking barefoot on the tile or terrazzo floors is bad and you will feel it when you get older.

SECOND STORY HOMES … are wonderful when you are young. When you get older, it will not be easy to walk up the stairs. If you can afford to install a chair or an elevator to lift you to the top floor, go for it!!!

LIST OF REPAIR COMPANIES……Keep a list of reliable and honest people who can repair or help you including a Roofing Company, Plumber, Electrician, Lawn Maintenance, Appliance Repair, Fence Company, a Reliable Handyman or anyone else that can help you in the future. This will be very important especially after a hurricane, flood, storm, etc. If they know you, they will come to you sooner than if you just called them for the first time.

★ Lack of planning on your part doesn't constitute an emergency on my part!!! ★

Do not buy the cheapest brand of anything!!! It will not last long and you will have to go back and buy the better brand. Buy the best that you can afford. Buying the most expensive brand doesn't mean it is the best!!! Check the Consumers Report!!!

Do not borrow any expensive items or tools from anyone!!! If it breaks, you will have to repair it or buy a new one. You should have either rented the item from a rental company or bought a new item for yourself!!!

Financial Elder Abuse

Illegal or improper use of funds, property, or assets of people 60 and older by family, friends, neighbors and strangers is punishable by law!!!

Internet Dating

Okay, here is my experience of Internet Dating. Before you decide to do that, I highly suggest you watch Lifetime Movie Network (LMN) on tv and learn a lot from it. I did that, done that and it was a nice experience but that was over 18 years ago. The internet was much safer before there was trafficking, perverts, etc. It is better to meet someone at church, at work or thru friends and family. It is much safer and less drama!!! Some men's profile has someone else's pic now which is usually a knock-out model, elaborate on their employment and looking for a Sugar Mama to take care of him. Some of these men are not even employed. I was very lucky with my experiences of my past and would never recommend it!!! I have even tried the Singles' Club which was a scam!!! They promise to hook you up for a fee of $1,000.00 which was over 28 years ago and take a video, shoot portrait pictures of you and then you go there to see if there are any matches that you would like to meet or check if there are any matches for you. Dream on!!! I mentioned that to my son, Keone, and he told me that I should have given him $1,000.00 and he would find me dates!!! It is more dangerous today so take my advice and stay away from these scammers!!! Watch LMN!!! That's the best advice I can pass on to you!!! Lots of men are lazy today and don't want to work and then after you date him, he wants you to pay for going out!!! My past relationship would expect me to pay every other time we went out!!! Don't fall for that!!! It's cheaper to go out with my friends and Dutch Treat!!! If he can't take you out and pay for the date, he can't afford you!!! I was in a narcissistic relationship and love being by myself. No more drama in my life!!! Red flag up, move on!!! Next!!!

Any woman before me is a mistake!!! Any woman after me is a downgrade!!!

Never be a prisoner of your past. It was just a lesson, not a life sentence!!!

If you're trying to suck up, it's working!!!

Whenever I meet someone and he says I've heard so much about you. I ask, was it all good things??? When the person says yes, I answer, It's all true!!!

I love with my heart until it comes to money and property…then my head takes over!!!

Be a COUGAR and date someone younger than you and make sure he is a legal adult!!! If you are an older woman, 60 or over, we are called JAGUARS!!! Call me JAG!!!

Most of my friends are younger than me…usually between 45 and 65 years old. You can learn a lot of the new fads, music, fashions and keep your mind with up to date things. I have always been that way since high school. Most of my boyfriends were younger than me. Guys my age are comfortable staying at home and are quite boring for me. Have fun with everyone and make your surroundings and life enjoyable!!!

Kanoe's Test

You are dating someone older and sooner or later, you start to kiss, hold hands, cuddle and get closer. This is my personal test for dating older men, good for older women who date and great for younger women who are attracted to older, rich men. After your date, you may end up somewhere where you have your own car so you can drive home and not depend on him. Lure him to sit on a chair without any arms. You sit across his lap (side saddle) and kiss him passionately!!! If you don't get elevated from his excitement, you still have your clothes on and you're a good girl!!!

You leave and the next time you talk to him, just say this is not going to work out!!!

You're done!!!

★ Don't forget to practice safe sex!!! Be sure you have your mask and a condom. Don't depend on him to bring it. A man's penis doesn't have a conscience!!! ★

Ahi Tuna Poke

Ingredients

2 pounds ahi, cut into bite size pieces

1/2 cup Maui Onion or Sweet Round Onion

1/2 cup chopped green onions

1/4 to 1/2 cup limu kohu (adjust to your liking)

2 TB. Ground Kukui Nuts (Inamona)

1 TB. Sesame Oil

1/4 to 1/3 cup Shoyu (Optional, Aloha Brand))

Hawaiian Ambrosia Salad

Ingredients

2-3 Bananas

1 (16 oz.) Container Sour Cream

2 Medium Oranges

4 cups Mini-Marshmallows

1 can (15 oz) or 2/1/2 cups Pineapple Chunks, drained

8-10   Fresh Lychees, Remove Seed

1/2 cup Shredded Coconut

1 (8 oz.) Cool Whip

1/2 cup Powdered Sugar

Instructions

1. Peel and cube bananas and oranges, then add pineapple chunks and lychees
2. Fold in cool whip and sour cream
3. Add mini-marshmallows
4. Toss coconut with powdered sugar and add to fruit salad
5. Chill and enjoy!!! So ono!!!

16

Things On My Bucket List

Pa'u Rider

$\mathcal{I}$n Hawaii, I used to dance on the floats that were in the Aloha Week Parades and the Kamehameha Day Parades. One year I decided I wanted to be a Pa'u Rider, the beautiful horseback riders who represented the different Hawaiian Islands and the Pa'u Riders that accompanied the Princess of the different islands in the Kamehameha Day Parade. I called my Aunt Harriet Magoon who was in charge of this parade and inquired about this. She told me to take horseback riding lessons so that I could qualify for it.

I took my first lesson, and they gave me a horse that moved too slowly. On my second lesson, I was given another horse that was a lot friskier. Well, the horse sensed that I was afraid and started to run faster as we were returning to the stables. That day the driveway entrance had ditches that were dug up for some pipes and this horse ran across the street and started up the driveway. Three men that were standing there saw me coming and one guy stopped the horse and another guy caught me as I flew off the horse. I hate to think what would have happened to me if these men weren't there. After this, my instructor wanted me to get back on the horse because if I didn't, I would always be afraid to ride a horse. I said, no way!!! I would only ride the horse that wouldn't move fast. Needless to say, after that incident, I called my Aunt Harriet and told her what happened and said that I was safer being a dancer on the float. Mahalo!!! I was intrigued by the floats that were decorated so beautifully. Later I wanted to build my own float which I did with my dance group in Orlando.

Parade Floats

I wanted to have a float in the Orlando Citrus Parade, so we got one of our dancers, Helen, who worked for Orlando Federal Savings, to sponsor us. That was the easy part. Now we had to get a flat-bed truck for our float, so we volunteered to do a Polynesian Show for the Army Division who were just on the outside of McCoy Base and got our flat-bed truck.

The next challenge was to get the Orlando Airport General Manager and Navy Commander, (since it was on Navy property) to allow us to decorate the float in a large empty hangar. This hanger was located on the west side of the airport off Tradeport Drive, that is now the Continental/ United Airlines Hangar used by Eastern Airlines Mechanics to park their extra airplanes to work on.

Hellen K., our Youth Center Director, got permission and we had the army deliver the truck to that large hangar which was empty. We decorated the float with lots of palmetto palm leaves and flowers and even made a rainbow. We decorated all night till about 2:00 am and as we were leaving an Eastern Airlines plane was towed into the hangar.

The next day, we had everyone, the dancers, drummers, King L. K. and Queen Hellen K. and Royal Court on the float. It was beautiful!!! All the dancers, drummers, families and friends helped us decorate the float and we were so happy and proud with our finished product. I could now cross this off of my bucket list!!!

At Christmas, we built and decorated a second float for the Orlando Christmas and Pine Hills Christmas Parades. Several companies asked if my dancers and drummers would ride and perform on their floats, and off course, we did it!!! So, besides our own float in the Orlando Citrus Parade, we were in the Orlando Christmas Parade, the Pine Hills Christmas Parade, and the Boy Scouts Parade. Wow, four floats in my lifetime!!! We loved that!!!

Doris Duke's Shangri-la

Shangri La is situated on a 4.9-acre oceanfront property in the exclusive Black Point residential neighborhood near Diamond Head. For those of you who are unfamiliar with Doris Duke, she was the billionaire tobacco heiress, known as Lucky Strike, and the Richest Girl in the World. She was the daughter of the wealthy tobacco tycoon, James Buchanan Duke, founder of the American Tobacco Company. My grand-aunt, Aunty Louisa, used to be Doris Duke's Head Housekeeper of her mansion on Diamond Head Beach, which could be seen from the parking area near the Black Point Lighthouse also known by the locals as the Submarine Races Parking Area. John G. was Manager of the Estate who was in charge of her mansion which had tennis courts, a large swimming pool which had a diving platform that would be elevated with musicians whenever Doris Duke had a party. Her beautiful and lavish mansion was decorated in Islamic-style. Whenever Doris Duke came into town, my Aunt Louisa, who had an apartment on the property and lived there full-time, would prepare the mansion for her arrival and hire maids, cooks and anyone else that were needed.

Whenever my aunt had a birthday, we would go to her apartment and celebrate. It was in 1958, when I first went there. My aunt showed us the kitchen which looked like a large kitchen for a hotel with all the pots and pans hanging from the top. Part of the house had the furniture all covered with sheets and I was impressed when she showed us the restroom that had a toilet that flushed silently. The large open room overlooking the cliff had a beautiful wall to wall aquarium that wrapped around the room with large salt water fish, eels and marine life. There was a playroom at one end of the pool and there was a man-made pool in the ocean that was blocked off with rocks to make it a private ocean pool for swimming. Today, you can pay to tour the mansion. You can actually see this home which has been updated on the internet under Doris Duke's Shangri La. I was very fortunate enough to see this when I was in college. That made me feel very special!!! My Bruddah and close friend & Keone's God-Father, Freddie P., later replaced John G. as the Manager of the estate.

Future Bucket List

1. WIN THE LOTTERY AND BECOME A MILLIONAIRE!!!
2. FLY IN EMIRATES FIRST CLASS SUITE
3. FRONT ROW AT BRUNO MARS AND BTS CONCERTS
4. GO ON A CRUISE WITH MY CHILDREN & STAY IN THE CONCIERGE SUITE!!!
5. ELLEN'S TWELVE DAYS OF CHRISTMAS WITH 2 FRIENDS
6. STEVE HARVEY'S FAMILY FEUD WITH MY FAMILY
7. FLY IN UA POLARIS MORE

HOPE I FILL THESE BUCKET LIST WISHES BEFORE I MAKE 87!!!

I have included two of my fave desserts below. Easy to make!!! Enjoy!!!

Lorrie Lee's Haupia for Party Group

4 quarts Liquid Coconut Milk

2 cups plus 2 TB. Cornstarch

2 cups heaping Sugar

- Dissolve cornstarch & sugar in Coconut Milk
- Strain into pot & cook over low heat
- Stir constantly until smooth & thickened with slightly increased heat
- Pour mixture into 9 x 13 pans.
- Let mixture cool & refrigerate to set.

Enjoy when firm!!!

Cinnamon Nuts

Mix 1 Egg White & 1 tsp. Water

- Pour over 1-pound pecans or walnuts
- Mix 1 cup sugar, 1 tsp. cinnamon, 1 tsp. salt. Mix with nuts.
- Roast on cookie sheet for 1 Hr. at 225 degrees.
- Turn every 15 min, then eat!!!

Salesman in China (Joke!!!)

A traveling salesman, Liam, was selling Cheer, the powdered detergent, in China going from house to house. He stopped at the first home and asked Meiling if he could demonstrate his cleaning detergent called Cheer. Liam asked Meiling to get him two buckets of water, (1) filled with warm water and (1) filled with cold water. He poured some cheer in the bucket with warm water and used the cold water bucket to rinse the clothing.

Liam asked Meiling to get a piece of clothing so he could demonstrate how Cheer could get her clothes so clean and she handed him a blouse. He started to demonstrate by washing the blouse in the bucket of cheer with a washboard and saying:

> *washee, washee, washee in the clean blue Chee-a (Cheer); rinsee, rinsee, rinsee in the wata (water) so clee-a (clear); Hold it up to your nose, with a satisfying smile on his face, smells like a rose.*

> *Liam sold his Cheer and continued to the next home.*

> *Liam continued his sales pitch to Li Ling who lived next door. Li Ling brought him a dress and he started his demo with:*

> *washee, washee, washee in the clean blue Chee-a; rinsee, rinsee, rinsee in the wata so clee-a;*

Put it to your nose, with a satisfying smile on his face, smells like a rose.

Liam was pleased to sell more Cheer.

Liam went to the last home on the block. He asked Mulan to bring him a piece of clothing and she brought him her underwear. Liam started to wash her underwear saying: washee, washee, washee, in the clean blue chee-a; rinsee, rinsee, rinsee in the wata so clee-a;

Put it to your nose, (he hesitates as he looks up to the ceiling with a frown on his face), smells like a..... washee, washee, washee in the clean blue chee-a!!!

Home Remedy
for Flu, Hacking Cough,
and Tight Congestion

1/4 tsp. Cayenne

1/2 tsp. Ginger Powder

1 TB. Apple Cider Vinegar

2 TB. Water

1 TB. Honey

- Dissolve Cayenne and Ginger in Apple Cider Vinegar and Water
- Add Honey and shake well

Take 1 tsp. as needed for cough. Works like a charm!!!

About Kanoe Kaye

*B*orn and raised in Honolulu, Hawai'i, Kanoe Kaye saw her home's post-war political and economic status was expanding, but women were still expected to limit their aspirations to roles as wife and mother. Kanoe made no secret that she wanted more, and her mother encouraged her to go for it!!! She made three wishes at nineteen: to travel to Japan with her Polynesian Revue troupe, to entertain on ships cruising the seas, and to travel while working for the airlines. *My Three Wishes* is a heartfelt memoir of pursuing her dreams and bringing joy to appreciative audiences around the world. See the pictures and hear the stories from Kanoe herself in this remarkable chronicle of sharing love and success with her children, a wonderfully poignant affirmation of Hawaiian "ohana," the idea that true happiness dwells within the family. Kanoe's story is both challenging and inspiring, an extraordinary journey that dares us to make and pursue wishes of our own.

Visit Kanoe's *My Three Wishes* fan page on Facebook for hundreds more photos!

Fresh Ink Group
Independent Multi-media Publisher
Fresh Ink Group / Push Pull Press / Voice of Indie

&

Hardcovers
Softcovers
All Ebook Platforms
Audiobooks
Worldwide Distribution

&

Indie Author Services
Book Development, Editing, Proofing
Graphic/Cover Design
Video/Trailer Production
Website Creation
Social Media Management
Writing Contests
Writers' Blogs
Podcasts

&

Authors
Editors
Artists
Experts
Professionals

&

FreshInkGroup.com
info@FreshInkGroup.com
Twitter: @FreshInkGroup
Facebook.com/FreshInkGroup
LinkedIn: Fresh Ink Group

Fresh Ink Group
FreshInkGroup.com

What drives a man to spend 26 years performing night after night? To persevere through a stifling tour bus, bad food, strange women, flared tempers, a plane nearly blown from the sky? Just how did that troubled military brat with a dream claw his way from dirt-floor dive-bar shows to the world's biggest stages? Aviator, author, and Country Music Hall of Fame drummer Mark Herndon lived that dream with one of the most popular and celebrated bands of all time. He learned some hard lessons about people and life, the music industry, the accolades and awards, how easy it is to lose it all . . . and how hard it is to survive, to embrace sobriety, to live even one more day.

Herndon's poignant memoir offers a tale at once cautionary and inspirational, delightful and heartbreaking, funny yet deeply personal. From innocence to rebellion to acceptance, can a man still flourish when the spotlight dims? Are true forgiveness, redemption, and serenity even possible when the powerful say everything you achieved somehow doesn't even count? That you're not who you and everyone who matters thought you were?

Mark Herndon refuses to slow down. So look back, look ahead, and join him on the trip. He's taking The High Road.

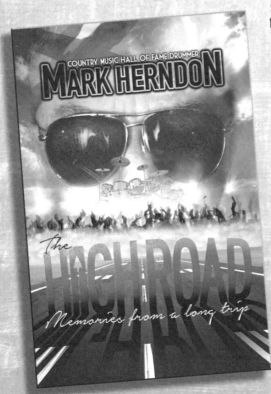

Fresh Ink Group
FreshInkGroup.com

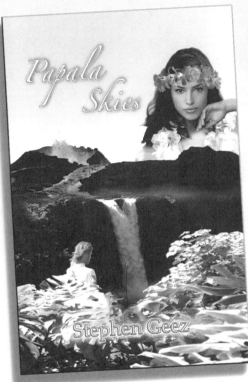

Chicago native Rochelle Du-Fortier likes to imagine the future, her world a series of picture postcards so vivid they sometimes seem real. When a foolish mistake at thirteen causes her mother's death, she's sent to a secluded Hawaiian valley, an outsider "haole-girl" among pidgin-speaking boys who hurl flaming papala spears under the full moon to summon her mother's spirit. After boarding school and a prestigious university back east, the ambitious young woman is torn between chasing new career opportunities, discovering her mother's heritage in a remote French village, and meeting obligations pulling her back to Hawaii.

On this island steeped in ancient mythology and modern superstition, Rochelle tests the possibility of sharing pieces of her life with those whose beliefs she barely understands and never intends to embrace. She dives the depths of a pristine coral lagoon, conceals bodies in a subterranean lava tube, and challenges the eruptions of a living volcano, even as she deciphers the truth about her mother's death and struggles to satisfy new debts born of old betrayals.

Papala Skies is the story of a young woman who makes all the right choices, only to find herself living an unexpected life. It is about the need to belong, and seeking one's own version of truth amid such differing cultures' responses to wrenching loss and abiding grief. It is about yearning for a sense of place, yet having to confront new ways to honor the love of family and friends.

Will Rochelle lose what matters most, or might she learn what the smart octopus already knows?

Fresh Ink Group
FreshInkGroup.com

The simple lives of everyday people in a mundane world prove extraordinary in this collection of 54 personal-experience essays by novelist Stephen Geez. The eclectic mix of memoir, commentary, humor, and appreciation covers a wide range of topics, each beautifully illustrated by artists and photographers from the Fresh Ink Group. Geez catches what many of us miss, then considers how we might all share the most poignant of lessons. *Been There, Noted That* aims to reveal who we are, examine where we've been, and discover what we dare strive to become.

Hardcover
Softcover
All ebooks

CPSIA information can be obtained
at www.ICGtesting.com
Printed in the USA
LVRC101454090721
691978LV00019B/243/J